PRESS PAUSE

AF871508

To all those people with whom I have had the privilege of sharing my journey.

PRESS PAUSE

AND TURN CHALLENGES INTO OPPORTUNITY

STEVE MACDONALD

echo
PUBLISHING

echo
PUBLISHING

An imprint of Bonnier Books UK
Level 45, World Square,
680 George Street
Sydney NSW 2000
www.echopublishing.com.au

Bonnier Books UK
4th Floor, Victoria House,
Bloomsbury Square
London WC1B 4DA
www.bonnierbooks.co.uk

Copyright © Steve Macdonald 2023

All rights reserved. Echo thanks you for buying an authorised edition of this book. In doing so, you are supporting writers and enabling Echo to publish more books and foster new talent. Thank you for complying with copyright laws by not reproducing or transmitting any part of this book by any means, electronic or mechanical – including storing in a retrieval system, photocopying, recording, scanning or distributing – without our prior written permission.

Echo Publishing acknowledges the traditional custodians of Country throughout Australia. We recognise their continuing connection to land, sea and waters. We pay our respects to Elders past and present.

First published 2023

Printed and bound in Australia by Griffin Press

MIX
Paper | Supporting responsible forestry
FSC® C018684

The paper this book is printed on is certified against the Forest Stewardship Council® Standards. Griffin Press holds chain of custody certification SCS-COC-001185. FSC® promotes environmentally responsible, socially beneficial and economically viable management of the world's forests.

Editor: Samantha Miles

Page design and layout by transformer.com.au

Cover designer: George Saad

NATIONAL LIBRARY OF AUSTRALIA

A catalogue entry for this book is available from the National Library of Australia

ISBN: 9781760688455 (paperback)
ISBN: 9781760688448 (ebook)

echo_publishing
echo_publishing
echopublishingaustralia

About the author

Steve Macdonald is an organisational psychologist and high-performance coach, and a keynote speaker in the areas of leadership, wellbeing and strategic cultural development. He has been privileged to work with individuals and teams across the industry spectrum, including professional services, mining, banking, engineering, education, healthcare and the public sector.

Contents

Introduction

Life happens. Celebrations, tragedies, pandemics ... not to mention all the other, more mundane, life experiences.

During such moments, opportunities emerge for us to pause, reflect on our life, and possibly make changes that will lead to a preferred future.

Often before we know it, it's five, ten, 15 years after an unexpected event in our lives that has momentarily stopped us in our tracks – and yet nothing has really changed in the long term. Sure, we have been busy: working diligently, doing our best as a partner, raising children, building friendships ... the list goes on. Although these are all worthy pursuits, occasionally we might find ourselves pausing to ask the 'Is this it?' question. 'Is this the sum of my life? Is this my reality?'

For some of us, this question arises only after we've stumbled into one of those all-too-rare introspective or reflective moments. For others, it has been nagging at us for a number of years. For others still, we arrive at a point in our lives where we feel we can no longer ignore the question.

The event that prompts this question might be the death of a loved one, a job loss, a relationship that no longer seems fixable, kids finally moving out of home, a financial calamity, unexpected prosperity or just a gnawing sense that there has to be something more. For many, the global pandemic was the impetus to ask this question.

After coaching many people through a life transition, I wrote this book as a guide to creating a structure around

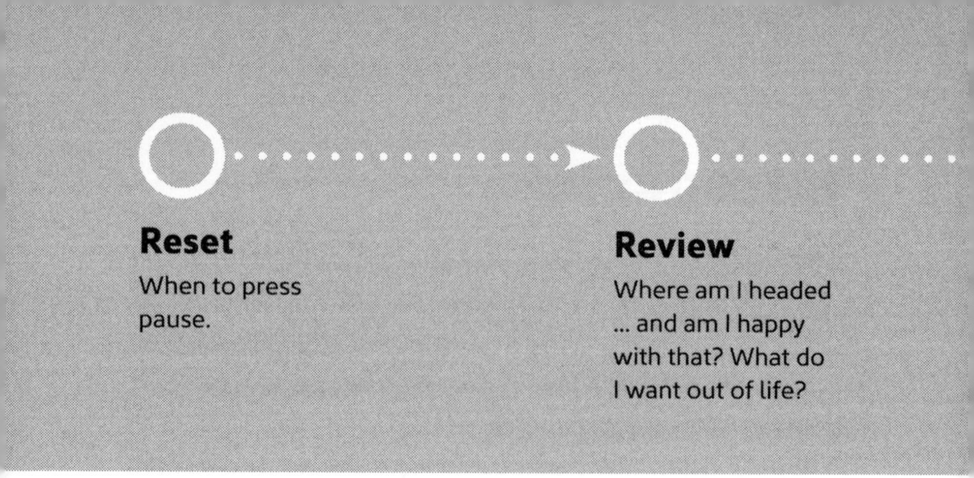

the thinking process we go through during such a time. As periods of transition can often feel confusing, frightening or challenging, it was written to help process what is important to you, and to prioritise those areas in your life that you may wish to recalibrate.

In my process I use four steps to break down and illustrate the different parts of the transition process:

- Reset
- Review
- Reacquaint
- Recalibrate.

The process can be drawn as above. We will use this diagram as we move through the book, a bit like a roadmap, so you can keep track of where you are in the process.

Within these steps there are five key questions that help us work through all the obstacles – conscious and unconscious – that are holding us in place and preventing us from moving easily from one phase of life to the next and/or creating a more fulfilling way of living. These are:

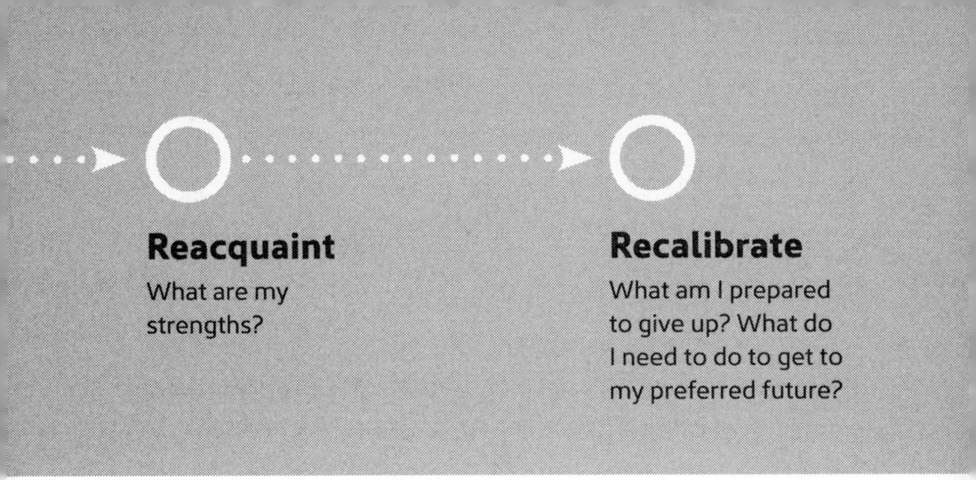

1. Where am I headed … and am I happy with that?
2. What do I want out of life?
3. What are my strengths?
4. What am I prepared to give up?
5. What do I need to do to get to my preferred future?

This process is a mix of ideas, based on the work I've done over the years helping people move through the transition process and on my own research. At the end of the book, you will find a transition plan template where you can reflect on each the five key questions to help you put in place a plan that will assist you to make the most of a transition period.

You can take notes as you read, answer the questions at the end of each section or take the time at the end to bring all your thinking together and put a plan into action. Alternatively, you can just read and reflect in your own way. My hope is that you can use this process to take your own pause in life and successfully find your pathway to a new and more fulfilling future.

Reset

Review

Reaquaint

Recalibrate

CHAPTER ONE

Reset: *'To set back to the initial state. To set anew in preparation for an update. To adjust after a system breakdown or setback.' This step is an opportunity to reflect on what you would like to reset as you move through your transition moment. It aims to help you understand more deeply exactly what the transition moment is for you.*

When to press pause

Opportunities for transition are happening all around us. Illness, an unfortunate accident, a new job, the ending of a relationship, the beginning of a relationship, children entering our lives or leaving our lives, the loss of loved ones, moving house ... All these events, whether joyful or tragic, share one interesting characteristic: they are all moments of opportunity.

Some of these occur by choice, while other changes are forced upon us by circumstance. Whatever the emotions they cause, the reality is that these moments offer opportunities for us to assess our lives and decide if we are happy where we are and if we are prioritising what is truly important to us.

Sometimes, these moments can be a gift that we only recognise at a later point. As Helen Keller once said, 'Although the world is full of suffering, it is full also of the overcoming of it.' Whether we feel we can do anything with these moments when they present themselves is another matter. The first challenge is recognising them as opportunities, followed by summoning our courage to take any action that may be required to put changes in place.

In this chapter, I am going to start walking you through a system of navigating change and a transition process. The first step, though, is to recognise when life has given you an opportunity to press pause.

Case study: **SAM**

TIME TO MAKE A CHANGE

Sam was approaching her 40s and was a very successful director and general manager of a division of a property-development organisation. Her life was comfortable. She had a great group of friends, and her second husband adored her. He was also the life of the party, and that suited Sam just fine as she loved entertaining and putting on a great event. Her relationship with a close relative was strained, but Sam felt that life was too short to get hung up on this.

Sure, she knew that she could be a perfectionist about her events, with every detail planned out to within an inch of its life. Sam didn't appreciate it when her parties took on a life of their own, and so made sure that all the people she invited would generally follow her rules. Getting into one of Sam's parties was an accomplishment and the wait list was long – just the way she liked it.

At work, her boss, Mark, had been making noises about selling off her part of the property-development business. She had a love–hate relationship with Mark. He had given her the opportunity of a lifetime ten years ago to own and manage a division of the business, which she had leapt at. During this time, she had managed to grow her division into the most profitable within Mark's portfolio, and so had done very well financially. However, this success had come at a cost to her relationship with her boss and the directors of the other divisions. They had been very open about their desire to remove her from the division, as they felt it was unfair that she was personally profiting so much.

Despite her success, Sam felt that it was time to make a change. Although she loved her lifestyle – which her financial success helped fund – she no longer trusted Mark and, in fact, could not even be in the same room with him. Friends had suggested moving on and starting over again – or even just retiring, as from a financial perspective she would never have to work again.

Sam came to me with a simple question: 'What should I do next?'

My response: 'It's time to press pause.'

As I lead you through each step of the transition process, I will be referring back to Sam's story, to demonstrate how one person navigated the particular circumstances of their own life change.

Recognising a 'pause' moment

One of the outcomes of the recent COVID-19 pandemic was 'the great resignation' from the job market or, as others have called it, 'the great realignment'. Essentially this was a cry for greater flexibility and control over our working lives in response to having collectively lived through such a monumental upheaval. It was the natural response to a significant life event. A response to grief that said: 'Life is more important than work and I want to take back control over what is truly important.' It was a time when we were all forced to 'press pause'.

As I write, there is great debate about the longevity of the pandemic and the reimagining of work by many people. I am not sure how this situation will play out in the long term, but one thing I have seen numerous times in people who experience traumatic or tumultuous events is that even though they may initially make changes, over time they drift back to their old ways.

As days turn to months and months to years, our lives generally go back to 'normal' ... or how they were before the traumatic event occurred. Interestingly, tragedy often does *not* provide the long-term impetus to be the agent of change that many of us assume it will. I don't make this statement as a criticism, but rather as acknowledgement of a pattern of behaviour I have observed in many situations.

How quickly our lives return to what they were before a major life event as the reality of day-to-day living kicks in!

There are, however, some people who experience what Professor Emeritus Richard Tedeschi calls 'post-traumatic growth' after a significant or tragic event. His research, published in the *Harvard Business Review* magazine in 2020, shows that 30 to 50 per cent of people experience personal growth after a traumatic event. Unfortunately, that means 50 to 70 per cent stay the same or deteriorate after a tragedy. Now, I'm an optimist, so I am more interested in the growth number and how that growth happens.

How quickly our lives return to what they were before ... as the reality of day-to-day living kicks in!

Your own employment story may be like that of a number of clients in senior positions who I have coached over the years. They have given their souls for a company, worked many long hours, made decisions to put work and colleagues first over family and friends, and then one day find themselves on the end of 'that' conversation. You know, the one where the CEO or a manager tells them how much the company appreciates them but now it's time to part ways. The typical reaction from my clients is: 'What now? I am not sure if I have the energy or motivation to reinvent myself or go on that journey all over again.'

The pain, anger or sense of wasted time experienced by people in this situation can be almost unbearable to witness.

It is not just the emotional toll of being told 'no thanks', it is also about facing the reality of decreasing personal finances and an increasing cost of living. I remember one client who'd had this happen. She decided now was the opportunity to take steps to pursue her passion, something she had never been confident to do while chained to her executive role. However, when I chatted to her a year later, she had given up her passion project and was back in a role similar to the one she'd had before. When I pressed her as to the reason, she explained that the lure of a significant wage was just too hard to shake, and she had decided that for now this was more important than pursuing her true interest.

Many of my clients also expressed the sentiment that while COVID-19 lockdowns gave them new freedoms and flexibility to work from home, they did so chained to the computer for up to 12 hours a day on video calls.

These are examples of transition, or reset, points in life that are too often ignored. Unless we are mindful and press pause, we do not see them as the opportunities they are. We may merely experience the effects of the major event for a while and then get back on with life as normal. In my experience, we rarely seize upon these moments and use them to propel us towards our preferred future.

If we can understand what happens in these moments and know what to do about them, then we can take advantage of the opportunities thrown at us and live the life we dream of. I believe that those people who experience post-traumatic growth have successfully pressed the pause button on their lives and made the most of the opportunity an event has provided.

My own employment pause

Like many people, I have experienced the opportunity to press pause.

One sunny spring day I was sitting in a leadership team meeting just staring out the window. I was completely devoid of energy or focus. I heard voices around me, but I seemed to be unable to tune into the conversation. I felt a little hazy (and no, I had not been drinking), and my thinking was definitely not sharp (okay, so that bit wasn't unusual). I had been working hard on a new project and burning the candle at both ends (nothing new there, either). There had been the usual internal politics required to implement a new plan, the normal argy-bargy of competing views and the standard guardians of the old way who seemed resolutely opposed to anything new or different.

I decided to call it a day and go home. I had left my front door keys somewhere (a clue as to what was about to happen), so I sat at the outside table and soaked up the sun while I waited for my wife to come home. I drifted between dozing off and staring into the sky for close to four hours, before she eventually came home and asked what was going on. I thought I was just tired. It turned out I was experiencing burnout.

While I didn't feel stressed, my doctor explained that I had all the symptoms (now, as a qualified psychologist, I understand he was right). I was physically and mentally stuffed (exhausted or weary is how the professionals would describe this). I was very cynical and had lost confidence in my abilities. Experienced over an extended period of time, these symptoms were all indicators of burnout.

The only way to recover from this was to stop!

I took a few weeks off to rest and think about life. However, as it turned out, I didn't think long enough because I soon jumped back onto the same treadmill, albeit in a different role. It was another year or so before I finally pulled the pin altogether. It became apparent the job wasn't the real issue.

The problem was that I was working in contradiction to what I wanted from life and my life's actual direction. As I tried to continue working and living like this, I failed to take the opportunity that had been offered to me to make a change. There were many things I still really liked about that job, but it was time to follow a different path – a fact that took me a year too long to realise.

Why do we not take advantage of these moments?

One of the main reasons we often *don't* take advantage of these moments is that we focus on *what* we want – rather than on *why* we want to do things differently and *how to make* that happen. All too frequently, you might hear people say things like: 'I want to be healthier', 'I want to spend more time with the family' or 'I want to leave work earlier', but these are desired outcomes, rather than specific actions that will lead to change.

We also tell ourselves stories about what we think we would like to be doing or who we would like to be, without even evaluating if we are on the right path for those things to happen. One thing I have learnt is that the only journey you can take is your own – I cannot walk the path of any other person's journey; although, often without realising it, that is exactly what I end up attempting to do.

In my life I have had several career transitions. After completing one year of engineering and then a three-year-teaching degree, I started my working life in a community services organisation and, while there, decided to study psychology. I had a year as a cleaner, as a worker in a meat factory, and as a manager in a local government council. I spent that time focusing on who I was and what I wanted out of life (and the answer was none of those jobs!).

I realised I enjoyed working with people but, more specifically, working with people to help them do things differently. While I enjoyed teaching, it honestly wasn't really something I could see myself doing long term. During my teaching career I realised that I value system change and got bored quickly working with the same people every day.

Like most people, I have autopilot switched on a lot of the time. And it serves a purpose. The regular rhythm that we get used to helps us maintain sanity, both at work and outside work. However, it is important that this switch is turned off occasionally, so we can recalibrate our direction to ensure we are living life in a manner that energises us.

If we don't take the time to do this, we will find that when opportunities to make a change occur, we will not be ready for them. If we try to take the skills, habits and mindsets that have helped us be successful in the past into the new post-transition phase of our life, we will usually discover that, rather than being helpful, they hold us back.

Transition phases provide us with a gift: the chance to stop and process. It is a gift too few of us accept. We recover from whatever happened, make a couple of murmured promises about learning our lessons, and get on with living.

Pressing pause is a state of mind

I'll never forget the night my wife and I received a knock on the door of our home while we were relaxing in front of the TV. It was a cold, wet night and we were curled up on the sofa. It had been another busy week, and unwinding with a pizza, a glass of wine and a movie in front of the fire was the perfect remedy.

My wife glanced out the window and noticed a police car had stopped outside our house. This was a rarity in our quiet neighbourhood, and we wondered why they were there. We ignored them until the knock on the front door came. A knock to inform us that a dear family member had unexpectedly passed away.

The calm of the evening was replaced by an inconsolable grief; a grief that is unexplainable to anybody who has not been in that situation before. In the days that followed, many questions were asked; memories shared; logistical arrangements about flowers, catering and the like were made; and lots of discussions about the meaning of life had.

To be honest, we continue to struggle with what happened that night. Wounds are still raw, tears still shed and a hole still exists in our hearts. No words or actions can completely heal us.

As is often the case in scenarios such as this, decisions are made by those who are left to live life more fully. These decisions are usually along the lines of holding loved ones closer, focusing on not just working for the money, spending time on 'what matters', and numerous other resolutions to live a more meaningful life.

Yet a few months later, many relationships go back to normal. When individuals have a job loss, relationship breakdown or other life-shattering moment they promise themselves they will focus on what matters and yet, after a few months, they are working just as hard as always, involved in a similar relationship pattern, or generally approaching life as they always have.

> Transition phases provide us with a gift: the chance to stop and process. It is a gift too few of us accept. We recover ... make a couple of murmured promises, and get on with living.

Why is this often the case? Are these events not enough reason for us to change? Are we making decisions in the heat of the moment that have no chance of lasting longer than a few hours or days? Are we actually okay with our lives as they are and don't really feel the need to change? Is this type of change beyond us? I think all these reasons have an element of truth to them, but I have also seen people who have changed their lives as a result of a life event – I have, my wife has, good friends have, colleagues have – and I firmly believe we all can.

We rarely have the chance to drop everything completely to press pause, because life continues whether we like it or not. While stories of those who take months off to traverse the back streets of the world to find themselves are inspirational, they can also be slightly annoying! Mortgages, families and other life responsibilities make these sojourns difficult for many people. At the same time, that doesn't mean we must accept life for what it is. These events are the perfect opportunity to press pause (even if just for a couple of days) to reflect on who we are and where we are heading.

Pressing pause is as much a state of mind as it is a pausing of life. It is a conscious choice to take stock and reflect on what is important. It is a deliberate decision someone makes because they want something different or better for themselves.

What if I don't like thinking too much about life?

There are those who love immersing themselves in deep introspection and reflection, spending time pondering life's great issues. There are also many of us who just want to get on with life, as there is 'too much navel-gazing already'.

I come across both types of people in my work (as well as those who fall somewhere between the two). I firmly believe that life is to be lived and that overthinking can lead to bouts of depression and inertia. However, I am also aware that we can go through life on autopilot without ever stopping to ponder some of those meaningful, larger questions. Unfortunately, in doing so, many people automatically accept their reality and don't question whether it is based on what is truly important to them.

So, consider this book an opportunity to do just that.

Reflection: the key to a life well lived

In my next session with Sam, whose story appears at the beginning of this chapter, I began with a question that I start most sessions with.

'So, how's the week been?'

Sam proceeded to tell me how pissed off she was with her boss, Mark, and that she felt life was just not stacked in her favour. It was what I would describe as a stream of consciousness rather than a well-thought-out description of her life. When I asked Sam what her plans for the future were, she told me all about an amazing party that she was planning for her partner and how this was what she really enjoyed in life. Now, I enjoy a party as much as the next person (maybe a little more), but it seemed to me as if Sam's whole life energy was directed at being a great party planner. I could also hear how stressful this party planning was for her, as everything needed to be perfect.

After listening for close to an hour, I interjected with what I thought was a simple question.

'What would a happy life look like for you?'

Sam stopped talking mid-sentence, stared at me and then said slowly, 'I have no idea, I have never stopped long enough to think about that.'

The superpower of reflection

Whatever our level of self-awareness, a pause or reset moment provides us with the opportunity to spend some time investigating or reaffirming why we do what we do. However, reflection on its own is not that useful. Spending too much time in your head thinking about the past and blaming yourself for what went wrong is what we call negative cognition and only adds to the emotional trauma you might be experiencing. Rarely does this cause us to move forward in a healthy manner – we usually just find ourselves completing the patterns of the past. (If this is the situation you find yourself in, then it might be time to consult someone who can help you move forward, such as a counsellor or a psychologist.)

A reflection process that is guided by asking the right questions is what we are aiming for. True self-awareness – to 'know thyself' – is about understanding your unique strengths and qualities and how they work together.

To do this, it is often useful to reflect on the following areas:

- Your values.
- Your personality.
- The strengths you bring to the world.
- The areas in life where you don't shine.
- The passions and life moments that light you up.

As Courtney Ackerman (mental health researcher for the State of California, USA, and author of numerous books on positive psychology) reveals in her 2020 article 'What is Self-Awareness?', true self-awareness or insight has been shown in many studies to be the precursor for successful relationships, leadership capability and general life success. This is where psychometric tools (e.g. personality assessments) can be useful, as not only do they pose questions about ourselves that we might not necessarily ask, they provide hard evidence for us to reflect on. The results they provide are often a surprise because, as a rule, we have never learnt to ask questions that actually dig deeper, beyond our everyday lives. As one of my friends said, 'I can't be expected to know what I don't know.'

> Reflection on its own is not that useful. Spending too much time in your head thinking about the past and blaming yourself for what went wrong is called negative cognition and only adds to the emotional trauma.

At this point I am sometimes asked the 'Does it really matter?' question. It comes in many different forms, as seen in the examples below:

'I have my job, life is comfortable, so does it actually matter whether I can articulate my values or what is important to me?'

'This reflection and thinking is theoretically nice, but it won't get me a job. It just feels like a waste of time.'

'It doesn't really matter if I recalibrate because at the end of the day my family or life will stay the same anyway.' (This has also been worded as, '*Well I might change but it's really just like changing the paint colour of my car – it might look different but, essentially, it's the same car.*')

Knowing ourselves deeply allows us to answer some important questions about our lives and to eventually plan, and take action on, a course of resetting, reflection and recalibration.

Some other extremely useful questions you can ask yourself to begin your reflection process include:

- What would I be happy doing?
- Who do I want to hang out with?
- What is important to me in life?
- What type of person do I wish to be known as?
- Why do I get angry when people behave in certain ways?
- What makes me laugh?
- What is within my control to change or adjust?

Reflecting on our basic psychological needs

We all have basic psychological needs for our wellbeing, and when these are not met, we can struggle. Unlike our basic *physiological* needs (shelter, water and food), which are essential for survival, our psychological needs enhance or decrease our sense of motivation, vitality, life satisfaction and overall general mental health.

In their book, *Self-Determination Theory: Basic Psychological Needs in Motivation, Development, and Wellness,* authors and researchers Richard M Ryan and Edward L Deci explored the basic psychological needs that we all share. Their findings, which became known as Self-

Determination Theory, provide a clue as to what helps us make a connection between who we are and the work we do. It is another useful way to guide our self-reflection, particularly when it comes to our work.

Self-Determination Theory says that all human beings have three basic needs:

- Autonomy – living a life and working in a place where we feel truly alive and can leverage our strengths.
- Competence – using and developing our skills.
- Relatedness – experiencing a feeling of connection and belonging with others.

As we move through life, our definitions of these three *psychological* needs often change (unlike our need for basic shelter, food and water). That's because they are directly related to our personal values. For example, we may seek casual employment when we are just starting out in life, to make time for study or social events. As we get older and gain more responsibilities (e.g. financial commitments, partners, housing), we might look for more stable employment that not only funds our life but hopefully mentally challenges and satisfies us enough to maintain it.

If we are not careful, though, we can become stuck on autopilot and miss opportunities to make changes that could enhance what we already have. And the problem with being on autopilot is that, over time, we very gradually and subtly lose focus of who we are and what makes us, *us*.

Are you ready to start?

Ideally, when we hit a moment in life that offers us an opportunity to press pause, we want to build habits that will help us make a sustainable change. Take some time to think through the questions below. You can write your answers in your own journal, capture your thoughts in the transition plan at the back of the book, or simply just think about your answers.

This is an opportunity to determine whether you are already in the starting blocks ready to begin the journey, or still making your way to the starting blocks. Either position is fine; just be honest with yourself.

- What is the transition moment you feel or think you are in right now?
- Where is the gift for you in this transition moment?
- What does embracing this transition moment mean for you?
- What would you like to believe, achieve or be once you have moved through this transition moment?
- Do you have any pressing deadlines or priorities you need to consider as you undertake this process?

• • • •

LET'S RECAP:

When to press pause

- Transition moments in life provide us with the opportunity to pause and think about where we want to go.
- Post-traumatic growth occurs when we emerge from a transition in a better place than when we entered it.
- Reflection is a superpower that allows us to take advantage of these transition moments.
- For reflection to be helpful we need to follow a process or framework – otherwise we run the risk of self-blame, and/or dwelling on the past, which may not assist us to move through the transition effectively.
- To transition effectively, we need our three basic psychological needs of autonomy, competence and relatedness to be fulfilled.

Reset

Review

Reaquaint

Recalibrate

Review: *'To critically and purposefully look over something again with the intention of implementing change as needed.' This step provides you with the opportunity to identify what is important to you in life, the journey that you would like to be on, and what shifts may be needed to get onto the life path that you desire.*

Where am I headed ... and am I happy with that?

Now that we have recognised a moment in our lives as an opportunity to pause and feel ready to undertake the process of undergoing a transition, we can move on to the next part of the process: analysing our reflections and reviewing what changes might be needed. To do that we can start with the first of the five key questions.

In my final year of high school, our class was taken on a rafting trip. It was the middle of winter and so we were instructed to wear wetsuits. I didn't have one and my parents didn't have the money to purchase one, so I went along just with my bathers and a T-shirt (long-sleeved of course ... I'm not an idiot). Our first safety test was to tread water for five minutes in a freezing cold river. For those in wetsuits (everyone but me), the task was tough but manageable.

One of the instructors took pity on me and threw me an oversized sleeveless wetsuit top. Apart from affording me some psychological comfort (and the instructor feeling like he was doing something to help the wimpy kid), that top didn't serve much of a purpose.

To complete the exercise, we had to float down some rapids. Not only was I freezing but now I thought I was going to die, as I had no buoyancy from the wetsuit like the others had. I remember feeling I had no control; simply accepting that once I was on my way, I would just have to continue to float to wherever I might end up (possibly out to sea, many miles away).

The instructor pulled me out at the end of the first set of rapids and explained that I did, in fact, have a choice. Once I had exited the rapids, I needed to take some control because he wasn't going to chase me all the way down the river. Apparently, he had 35 other teenagers to look after. He explained that I had to make an effort to get to one side of the river, rather than just float aimlessly. He then made me walk back up to the top of the rapids and repeat the exercise until I could successfully get to one of the riverbanks.

Harsh exercise, but a nice analogy for life.

At some point many people simply resign themselves to the movement of their life; although not happy with their direction, they just 'float' along with it. There is effort required to realign with your life values and get back on track. This often begins with the realisation that you have drifted off the track you want to be on.

After sharing the above story with Sam, whom we first met in Chapter One, I said, 'The obvious question to ask is: "Which track are you currently walking on?"'

Sam said, 'I am not sure what you mean by this.'

I responded with a series of further questions to help Sam with her reflection on her current life path.

- Are you happy with the direction your life is headed?
- Are your close relationships providing fulfilment?
- Is your financial state what you would like it to be?
- Is your career heading the right way?
- Are you happy with the state of health you are in?
- Do you have a circle of friends you enjoy?

After a pause, Sam said, 'It's not that simple. I have different answers for each of the questions. My relationship is just where I want it to be and I love my current friends. Some I have known for years, and some have only just entered my world. My financial position is very solid and, in fact, I never dreamed that I could have it this good. I am very blessed.'

> There is effort required to realign with your life values and get back on track.

'Of course,' I replied. 'There are no right or wrong answers to any of these questions. The answer is the one you are happy with. This might sound like an obvious statement, but the truth is, if you are happy with just a few good friends then you are on the right track for friends. However, if you are not happy with the state of your career, then maybe you need to think about what needs to change.'

'Well, that's the problem,' said Sam. 'I have never stopped to think about my career and my life trajectory. I have never felt like I have had to until this moment.'

The important question to ask then is this: *Have you resigned yourself to the fact that your life at the moment is all it can be?* This question involves comparing what is important to you and what your life currently looks like. We call this a gap analysis.

How wide is the gap?

A very wise person once told me if you want to know what's important to a person, look at what they spend their money on and how they spend their time.

What would these two things say about you? Are they an accurate reflection of what's important to you?

All of us have some gaps in our life. Maybe I have a great relationship with my wife, but I have let my health go and I need to close the health gap. Maybe my peers at work would describe me in a positive light but those who report to me may have other things to say. I might need to work on my work relationships gap. Maybe I am caring for the environment in a manner I am proud of, but I spend little time with those who are closest to me. I might need to consider that gap, also.

> A very wise person once told me, if you want to know what's important to a person, look at what they spend their money on and how they spend their time.

There is no correct answer to any of the questions I posed to Sam. This is not about everyone being the same or having the same values; it is about asking ourselves whether we are okay with the gaps we have discovered. I have found that the best way to answer this question is to be clear about our motivation for doing certain things and what we want out of life.

If you truly desire a closer relationship with your family, but spend all your time in work-related activities, then there will be a gap. You could justify this by saying it is a 'just for a while' decision, and compensate by investing in great holidays or scheduling 'quality' time with the family; but if the gap is greater than you would like, then you need to be honest with yourself about it.

One reason we may keep floating down the river of life is that we feel there's no way back to our ideal, no way to close the gap. We feel powerless against the raging current, so we just float along and wait for a hand to reach in and pull us out.

Thankfully, the reset moment you are in *is* that hand.

Sure, it may feel like the odds are stacked against you. For example, while you might like to close a relationship gap, the financial needs you have just won't allow it. The reality is that you have to put in the hours to earn the money to be able to afford your house and lifestyle. The question here, then, is not about your family or job, but how important *the gap between the two* is to you. At this stage in the process, we are just identifying the gaps. Further along in the process we will explore how important those gaps are to you.

I would like you to take a moment to look more closely at the gaps that may exist between where you are right now and where you would like to be.

Unlocking the future (by unpacking the gaps)

Let's return to my session with Sam. After she had paused for a few minutes and reflected on what she wanted out of life, she said, 'I've never really thought about what my life would look like if I was happy and I wouldn't even know where to start. How do I even figure this out?'

Reflecting on the gaps in her life required Sam to think about the core dimensions of what makes a life well lived. The set of questions I have listed below are some I have learnt to ask over the years, but they are by no means exhaustive.

For this exercise I encouraged Sam to keep a note of her answers so that we could unpack her thinking next time we met. I encouraged her to truly reflect on her responses, write them down and add to them over the next week or so. I explained that she may find that her initial response changed as she continued to dig deeper. I explained to her that this is where the pathway for her new life would start to emerge.

How to identify gaps

The following questions are the ones that I gave Sam. You might like to capture your responses in the transition template at the back of the book if you would like to keep a record.

How does what you do in your work line up with what you want out of life (or your 'why')? Do you need to make a real stretch in logic to align your why with what you do for a living? If you could step into another type of work tomorrow, what would it be? Is there a gap between what you would step into and what you are doing now? What are you doing to close the gap?

How would you describe your closest relationships? We are made to be in relationships with others. When you think of your closest relationships (i.e. partners, family, friends) what would you like these to look and feel like? What do they currently look like? Do you feel like you are able to be the best version of yourself? What is the gap? Are you okay with that? What is your part in this gap? What could you do to close the gap?

Who are your friends? I heard once that we are defined by our closest friends. I don't mean your social media friends but rather those you rely on and who rely on you for social connection. Do you spend your time regularly with these friends or do you find yourself foregoing time with them for colleagues and other pressing needs? Are there people you would like in this group who you have drifted away from over the years? What would you like your friendships to look like? What could you do to close this gap?

What is the state of your physical health? While it would be nice to be as toned as a Greek god and to be able to leap small buildings in a single bound, I am talking about your health, rather than how you look or your physical abilities. Are you at an ideal weight for your body size? Is your nutrition intake fuelling your brain and body? Are you moving a few times a week (and I mean a little more vigorously than the daily commute to work)? Are you getting seven to eight hours of quality sleep a night? If you could paint a picture of health for you, what would that look like? What are you doing to close the gap?

What is your personal impact? How would those you live with, work with, play with and spend time with describe you? If you have a leadership role, how would those who report to you describe you? How do you know? How would your customers describe you? Is this okay with you? What are you doing to close the gap?

A word of friendly warning here: If you are completely happy with the way others describe you then either you are not listening to honest feedback all that honestly or you have decided that you are perfect the way things are (a slippery slope either way).

Do you have awareness of your spiritual world? A paper published by researchers from the University of Malaysia in 2016 indicates that there is a spiritual component to all human beings. We all describe and experience that differently, but nevertheless it is still part of us. Often people say they are too busy to contemplate spirituality, or would like to give attention to more practical matters of their life first. I like to think of the spiritual component of my life as the fuel that enables me to deal with the other pragmatic issues. How much time do you allocate to your spirituality? Do you participate in retreats, journalling, meditation, prayer, reading, volunteering or some other activity that you regard as a 'spiritual' practice? How much time and energy do you give to this area of your life? Are you happy with how it stands? If not, what could you do to close the gap?

Are you financially where you wish to be? Are you living a life held back by your financial situation or does your financial situation enable you to live the life you wish to live? This is not about having the right amount of money but more about the attitude you bring to your finances. Are you creating a solid base? Are you able to live generously? Are you able to enjoy the quality of life you want? Where is the gap for you? What are you doing to close this gap?

What is the state of your emotional health? Are you able to display emotional resilience or do you find that life overwhelms you? How do you respond when things don't go your way? Are you able to see a way forward or do you default into negative self-talk or pointing the finger? Where is the gap for you? What are you doing to build your emotional health? The status of your emotional health and resilience will determine your pathway forward.

How did you go? Before we begin to investigate our answers, let's take a few moments to pause and reflect on the gaps that exist in our world. Did you notice something about each of the gaps? Would you like to close some of these gaps ... but don't have the energy or inclination to do so? What would be the consequence of not closing these gaps?

When I asked Sam how she had gone with the above questions she replied, 'That was super tough! I had to think about all areas of my life and I realised that there are some significant gaps in what I want out of life and how I am living my life now.'

> Sometimes we can identify a gap but lack the energy to do anything about it.

Like Sam, if you looked closely at your answers, you were probably faced with the reality that there are some things you need to change. You possibly also found yourself thinking that if some external factors shifted, you could close that gap more effectively. It is normal human behaviour to play the 'What if?' game. What if I was suddenly to come into a large amount of money? What if I could start all over again? What if my life was easier? What if my boss noticed my talent? What if that idea suddenly took off and I didn't have to struggle so much? What if ...?

There is nothing wrong with having this conversation with yourself every so often and dreaming a little (in fact, I would encourage it). The problem emerges when we wait for the 'What if?' to happen before we work on closing the gap. There is usually little point waiting for that 'magic pill' to fix our problems – the gap rarely closes of its own accord. It is amazing how opportunity strikes those who have been working hard or how often an 'overnight success' follows many failed attempts and years of hard work.

I know some of you will be thinking: 'That's easy for you to say, Steve, but I have been working hard for a period of time and the gap doesn't appear to be closing.'

Life is often not as simple as some would make it out to appear. Sometimes we make one adjustment and everything changes, while other times we do everything in our power and nothing changes. Sometimes when we look at others, we wish we had life as easy as they do or that things worked out for us as smoothly as it seems to for them. Sometimes we can identify a gap, but lack the energy to do anything about it.

I have learnt over the years that nobody has everything easy and that we should not be fooled by appearances. All of us have areas we struggle with, despite how it may appear on the outside. I have also learnt that sometimes we make things harder for ourselves when we seek to close our identified gaps, because we have unspoken non-negotiables. These are beliefs that we are not prepared to let go of. There are many reasons we may hold these, but the bottom line is that we are not prepared to change them. Sometimes we are not even aware that we have them.

Why do I put others first ... even when it is to my own detriment?

Sometimes we can identify a gap but lack the energy to do anything about it. One common reason for this is that we have put our own wellbeing last for too long.

There are many reasons why we may put other people first. Our children are dependent on us for guidance and nurturing; our work colleagues need a helping hand; our friends need a shoulder to lean on, or a sick family member needs you to take care of them.

There is nothing terribly wrong with that picture; that is life as normal, we don't live in a bubble and so must make time for others. And if we have been blessed with good fortune, even if we have worked incredibly hard for it, we often feel we are supposed to look after those around us.

And yet ...

We often give our energy to others at a rate that is to our own detriment. We may even start to resent all that extra work, yet we soldier on until it gets too much. We become worn down and realise our sense of self has disappeared. Our wellbeing suffers, our health deteriorates, but we continue to put ourselves last because it's the 'right' thing to do.

What's happening here?

We are experiencing a form of personal hypoxia.

I spend a substantial amount of my life sitting on planes, and I have heard the oxygen mask briefing too many times to remember. It is presented in many ways – some creative and some ... well ... anyway, it boils down to if the plane starts to crash and the oxygen masks drop down from the ceiling, put yours on first before helping any small children and others around you.

While it seems rather obvious advice, I think I would respond like most people in an emergency. Our default reaction would be to help any small children around us before putting on our own mask.

But here's where it gets interesting.

While it is human nature to help small, innocent people in times of emergency, this very basic instinct could, in fact, cause serious damage to those we are trying to protect. It is an unintended consequence of kindness.

> I have learnt over the years that nobody has everything easy and we should not be fooled by appearances.

When we go too long without oxygen, we experience something called hypoxia. Hypoxia impacts cognitive functions and can cause confusion, blackouts and even brain damage. The reason I need to put on my oxygen mask first is to ensure I have my faculties about me so I can truly help those innocent younger people. I can even cause unintentional damage if I don't have my faculties about me.

Likewise, when we neglect ourselves by giving our energy to those around us, we often experience a version of hypoxia. We neglect to put on our wellbeing oxygen masks because we just don't have the time, there are so many other demands; or the old excuse … I will help myself when:

- things quieten down
- I am less busy
- they get their lives sorted
- my children don't need me anymore.

I call this the 'When …' argument.

The problem with the 'When …' argument is that this desired end-state never fully eventuates, so we spend our entire lives trying to help others without wearing our oxygen masks. Not only do we become less effective (which we may admit to ourselves in quieter moments), we also become increasingly less well.

Taking a moment to reflect on the gaps in our lives is also the perfect time to stop and put on our oxygen mask. As part of that, we need to think about the reasons we forget to wear it (or why, when we *do* remember to put it on, it always seems to fall off). More importantly, it is the time to reflect on the cost of neglecting our oxygen mask – both for ourselves and for those around us. Learning to know ourselves, and recognising the signs that tell us our mask is falling off, are so important for us to stay at our best.

LET'S RECAP:

Where am I headed ... and am I happy with that?

- Successful transitions require us to be honest about the direction our life is taking and whether that is the direction we want for ourselves.
- All human beings have gaps in their life between what they say is important and how they are actually living. Being honest about these gaps is the first step to a successful transition.
- There are no magic pills or secret solutions that close the gaps. The longer the gaps have been in your life, the more focus and persistence will be required to close them. This focus on closing the gaps is worth the reward.
- It is not selfish to focus on yourself and what you want out of life. In fact, the irony is that when you are aware of the gaps and working to close the ones that are important to you, you become a better version of yourself and you will attract the right people into your world.
- There is no perfect time to begin the process; starting now is as good a time as any.

What do I want out of life?

Let's move on to the second of our five key questions in our transition system.

At the start of our third session, Sam seemed to be a lot more upbeat than previously. 'You know,' she said, 'I feel like all this reflecting might actually be useful.

'I haven't really been keeping a journal but I am thinking about those questions a lot. I think I am starting to become a lot clearer about what I am happy with and where I may need to make some adjustments.'

'Great,' I replied. 'So, what do you want out of life?'

Sam's first response was, like most people's: 'Well, like everyone, I guess, I just want to be happy.'

'I want to be happy is not specific enough,' I told her. 'We all want to be happy, but from my experience my footy team makes me happy but doesn't have the same impact on my wife. A good bottle of wine makes me happy, while a good photo opportunity makes her happy. My dog is just happy whenever anybody will throw his ball (doesn't make him such a great guard dog).'

'What do I want out of life?' seems like a simple enough question, but it is one that people find difficult to answer. However, it is an important question to ask to help you determine your focus. And focus is what will help you move in the direction you want to take.

Over the next hour, Sam and I explored how to discover our focus by discussing further questions such as:

- What gets you out of bed every morning?
- What excites you?
- What would you do if you had the ability to focus on anything you wanted to?
- At the end of your life, what impact would you be happy to have left behind?
- What do you *not* care about?

Some further ideas to discuss that could help you pinpoint your focus are:

- What will make me happy?
- What is success from my viewpoint?
- What type of relationships do I want?
- What would cause me at the end of my life to say, 'That was a life well lived'?

What makes for a life well lived, for you?

The power of feedback is amazing. As a youngster I created a toy radio out of cardboard and tape. I was obviously very proud of my handiwork. I mean, it looked okay; it didn't actually work but it looked like the radio transistor I was trying to recreate. As a ten-year-old I was incredibly proud of myself and showed off my 'masterpiece' to anyone who was around.

One well-meaning adult told me that I would make a great engineer, and for some reason that piece of positive reinforcement stuck. I went through the rest of my schooling fixed on the idea that I was going to become an engineer.

Now, I was a teenager who loved sports, fun and music, so it's not like I was completely focused on being an engineer. But in those times when I thought about what I wanted to do when I left school, that was my answer. I even 'faked' my Year 12 career guidance assessment so that 'engineer' was one of my top three career choices.

However, after one year of engineering I quit and went into teaching, followed by psychology. Two disciplines that are as far removed from engineering as possible. (They both involve working closely with people, for a start.)

> Knowing what we want out of life is important. It provides us with a focus. It enables us to start moving in a consistent direction, rather than being like a bird flitting here and there.

Today I work with a lot of engineers; I have a good mate who is an engineer and a brother who is trained as one. I have one simple observation on the subject: I would have made a terrible engineer.

Details are not a strength of mine, nor is digging deep to see whether the design is correct. I don't have a desire to fix everything and solve problems, and I can't sit still long enough to focus on the intricacies of how something is working. The world has been spared having to ride in, climb on, live within, or use anything that I have designed or built. This is definitely a win–win situation for all involved!

What happened?

I wasn't starved of positive reinforcement as a kid. I did well at school and could have taken on any career I wanted. But after receiving the aforementioned positive feedback, I decided I wanted to be an engineer – and then everything I did seemed to reinforce that I was on that particular track. There is a neurological reason for this. It's called the reticular activating system.

At the base of our brain stem lies a cluster of nerve cells called the reticular activating system (RAS). We are constantly bombarded by countless stimuli vying for our attention, and it is the job of the RAS to determine what gets noticed and what goes unnoticed. Like a radar system, the RAS determines what makes a blip.

As I had decided I wanted to be an engineer, my RAS radar picked up on events and stimuli that reinforced this world view. I am good at maths (tick); I like to be practical (tick); I sometimes find people annoying (tick). (Sorry, that was a cheap shot.) The point remains that what I thought I wanted was being reinforced by what I saw around me.

In life there are those who have decided what they want but are a bit like me and engineering. What they think they want has been reinforced by others or is based on faulty data. (You only have to watch a talent show to see some really great examples of this!) Other people have no idea, and stress about not having the answer. Sometimes they stop living and simply exist, waiting for a beam of light from above to provide direction. Some people never want to stop long enough to answer the question at all but find themselves at some point existing rather than listening.

Knowing what we want out of life is important. It provides us with a focus. It enables us to start moving in a consistent direction, rather than being like a bird flitting here and there.

Discovering your passions helps pinpoint your unique strengths

We all have those things we get passionate about, and the world needs that. Someone once said that there are almost as many causes in this world as there are people. But that doesn't mean we all have to be passionate about the same things. There are many important issues I could get excited about but, to be honest, I am glad that someone else gets excited about them ... they just don't float my boat. (Of course, when we are passionate about something, we generally find like-minded people and then wonder what is wrong with the rest of the world.)

Understanding what you are passionate about is an insight into what you want out of life.

I love my dog but I am not passionate about animals. I understand the need to have a healthy and sustainable environment, but I am not passionate about it. I *am* passionate about things to do with people, so it is no surprise that I get excited about helping people unlock their own potential. I also love helping groups of people to be able to function effectively in order to achieve their dreams and ambitions. I am passionate about people understanding themselves at a deeper level to unleash potential ability, but I am not that interested in spending hours and hours with someone in therapy (and trust me, that really *is* a win–win situation).

When I think about my own sphere of influence, it is at the macro level. I believe in individuals, but I want to influence global groups. I care about people getting their lives back on track, but I want to motivate others to get involved, provide organisational excellence and fund those who dedicate their lives to working at the coalface. I am not better or worse than someone who does want to work one-on-one with people, I just understand my passions and therefore what I want out of life.

> Reset moments can be painful because the state of 'comfort' is disrupted. What we do in this moment is important: it can set us on a new path or we can re-enter a state of entropy and circle back around.

This is not an excuse to only focus on things I am comfortable with; rather, it's an acknowledgement of where I can bring value. My ambition to be able to fund others to make a significant difference is huge and, to be honest, a little scary, as my ambition outweighs my current reality. That's okay, though, because it provides a filter for everything I do: writing, speaking, consulting, coaching and living.

Ambition is not a dirty word ... it is vital for our health!

Our ambitions might vary but we all have them. Some people long to run organisations, others to have a warm, loving family, some to climb mountains and others to be part of a sporting club. Looking forward, and with a desire to have a better future, is important for all human beings. If we are not looking forward, then we are in a state of entropy.

The second law of thermodynamics tells us that when systems are left alone then entropy increases – they become messier, less efficient and break down. As humans we have the same tendency. When we get comfortable with life exactly as it is or give up trying to move forward, we begin to move backwards and can begin to break down.

Sadly, sometimes we discover this fact when it is too late; for example, towards the end of our lives, or when a relationship has become irreparably damaged, or when we realise the career ladder we have been climbing was leaning against the wrong wall, or when our health has deteriorated to a point that requires major intervention.

Reset moments represent the exact opportunity to recognise whether we are in a state of entropy, because they are a shake-up of normal life. These moments can be painful, because the state of 'comfort' is disrupted. What we do in this moment is important: it can set us on a new path, or we can re-enter the state of entropy and circle back around.

Of course, life being full of many moving parts, it means we may well be moving forward in some areas but be in a state of entropy in others. This is why stopping and asking the 'What do I want out of life?' question at regular intervals is important.

How do I find the strength to change?

After talking through life passions and ambitions for an hour, Sam said: 'I think I get it, but how do I find the strength to change those areas of my life where there are gaps?'

Generally, the answer to this question is that a deep-seated reason is needed for there to be sustainable change.

Losing weight because you want to be healthy may not be a strong enough motivator. Losing weight so you look good for that wedding you have been invited to will have some success, possibly, but that will stop after the wedding. Losing weight because you want to play a significant part in your children and grandchildren's lives is possibly a stronger motivator. However, it is important to say here that all our motivations are deeply personal – and so what motivates one particular person will be different to what motivates another.

> As you are going through the change, there will be times ... let me repeat ... *there will be* times when you will want to quit and go back to the old way. That is normal and it is part of the process.

For our motivations to be sustainable and long-lasting, they need to be based on deep-rooted incentives.

I said to Sam: 'Changing jobs because you don't like the current boss or because you feel trapped will rarely have long-lasting impacts. Changing jobs because you realise that you have unused gifts and you wish to step out and use those strengths will be a stronger driver.'

'Essentially,' said Sam, 'You are talking about my "why".'

In short, yes. Your 'why' must be enough to keep motivating you through the pain and uncomfortableness of change. As you are going through the change there will be ... let me repeat ... *there will be* times when you want to quit and go back to the old way. This is normal, and it is part of the process. Our reason for changing must be personal and deep enough to sustain us when we want to go back to the old way that feels comfortable.

> If you are changing only because people are telling you that you need to, then that will not have a lasting impact ... ultimately you need to have a 'why'.

Changing for someone else's reasons is rarely effective or long term. If you want to lose weight because you think that is what is required by others, if you want to change jobs because the boss is not someone you enjoy working for, or you wish to enter a relationship so you are not lonely, then you will probably circle back to your same old problems.

If you are changing only because people are telling you that you need to, then that will not have a lasting impact. Additionally, just because you get motivated by a great book, inspirational story or hearing a fantastic speaker is also not reason enough to change.

These can all be great catalysts but ultimately you need to have a 'why'. A 'why' that is personal, a 'why' that is yours, a 'why' that you truly believe in, a 'why' that is completely owned by you ... even if others don't get it. In fact, if others don't get it or look at you with bemusement when you explain your 'why', then you are probably on the right track.

Sometimes our whys have to be a little out there or different to what people expect from us. Then it is different enough from the normal to be yours.

After listening to this, Sam said, 'This sounds like it could be tough!'

'Yep,' I replied, 'these are the hard yards. However, the result can be a life that you had only dreamed of.'

Time to reflect

I believe that for deep change to happen, it is important to stay in this space of reflection for a little while. The space of truly understanding your why and to review why change is important to you. It is out of this time that the new you will emerge.

One of the reasons we don't make the transition from reset to recalibration effectively and find ourselves back in the same space as before is because we skip this stage or, at best, pay lip service to it. A seed has all the potential that is needed for a plant to begin its life. It is, however, from the planting of the seed, fertilising, watering and allowing the seed to germinate properly that the plant emerges.

If we cut corners with this natural process, the plant becomes weak or doesn't grow at all. Of course, the right amount of water can expedite the process, whereas drought will slow the process. The 'water' for our process is accepting your value and understanding who you are. The deeper this knowledge and the greater your acceptance of it, the more quickly this next stage can happen ... but it needs to take its course.

Some of us are very comfortable to sit in this space and stay there, while others find it very uncomfortable. Below are some questions that will help you to think about your passions and motivations for change.

- What floats your boat? What do you care about? What would you like to see done differently in your family; your relationships; your work; the world?
- Describe how you would like your life to be in a few years' time (or whatever time span applies in your situation). What would you be doing? Who would you be around? What would you not be doing? How would life be different to what it is now?
- If you could change something right now about your reality, something that is in your power to change, what would that be?
- Why would you want to change that?

LET'S RECAP:

What do I want out of life?

- Your change reason must be your own. Change that is motivated by others is rarely successful for the long term.
- We all have our own version of what it means to live a good life.
- Those things in life that create passion in you are a clue to what a well-lived life could look like.
- Having a focus for our life provides us with some clarity about how we want to come out of a transition moment.
- Ambition is simply having the courage to dream about what we want out of life and to take steps to move in that direction.

Reset

Review

Reaquaint

Recalibrate

CHAPTER THREE

Reacquaint: *'To take the time to rediscover something or get used to something again.' This step focuses on rediscovering who you are and learning about your unique value that will sustain you through the transition. 'Reacquaintance' is all about living life with your unique fingerprint.*

What are my strengths?

'That's a brave decision, Steve.'

There have been a few times in my life when I have heard this. The most recent was when I left the organisation I was leading at the time to start up a new business. Didn't I know that leaving the security of a well-paid job, where I was doing a lot of what I loved, was risky? Didn't I know that most start-ups fail? Didn't I realise all the blood, sweat and tears that would be involved?

I did.

I also knew I had a dream, and that I had strengths that were being under-utilised. I knew there was a big part of myself that was not living. I could complain about this, grow miserable, hope for a better future ... or I could take action.

So, action was what I took.

Then a global pandemic hit the world. Devastating lives and, less significantly but still important to me, making it tough to run your own business.

Fortunately, this step proved to be one of the best of my life. Sure, there were setbacks and lots of struggles, but success has followed; success that, to be honest, I still feel is undeserved. Yes, I and those around me worked hard for this success but, as I look back, it only happened because I was finally using my gifts.

As I reflect on my life, I see this pattern emerge every time I made one of those brave decisions.

Successful change tends to follow when we understand and step forward into our unique value.

We have now come to the third of our five key questions. In order to discover your own personal strengths and values, we are going to spend a bit of time digging deeper into what makes you tick. True, life-changing, sustainable transitions generally don't occur unless we are courageous enough to be honest about who we really are and what is important to us.

Who am I?

Your identity is not some abstract concept that is nice to figure out if you get the chance. Understanding your identity is pivotal to recalibrating your world.

Your identity is how you define yourself. It is who you feel you are at your core. It is built from the stories you tell yourself about the experiences you have. These stories are influenced by your personal values, your upbringing, belief systems and your own personal wiring.

Shifting identity is not about getting a new wardrobe, changing the bands you listen to, supporting a new footy team or moving to a seaside location. These may be the *result* of shifting your identity, but they are not in and of themselves an identity shift. I have seen many people engage in such superficial activities because they are not happy with their life or find it unfulfilling. More times than not, after making such a shift, they will need to go through another one because they haven't asked or reflected on the fundamental question: 'Who am I?'

> Successful change tends to follow when we understand and step forward into our unique value.

Sometimes, however, it is easier to change the superficial every so often rather than dig a little deeper to find out the real version of yourself. 'Shifting deckchairs on the *Titanic*', quite a common saying, is a good way to describe this action, and is always easier than dealing with possibly deep-seated underlying issues. But we all know what eventually happened to the *Titanic*!

I know those of us who are action-oriented, achievement-focused and just want to get on with life probably feel they don't have the time, nor the inclination, to stop and deep-dive. However, transition moments such as a change in job, death of a loved one, new additions to our family, relationship breakdown or new relationships, children moving out or a change of address are all perfect opportunities to spend a few moments reflecting on who we are at a deeper level.

What does pizza have to do with our identity?

I remember driving to a friend's place before I had a maps app on my phone. I had to rely on my memory of the directions I was given, as well as a cursory glance at a road directory (yes, believe it or not, navigation used to happen without a phone!). The problem was, I kept circling past the same pizza place, called 'Rocco's Pizzas', which was located on the intersection of two main roads. I knew something wasn't right, but I couldn't figure out what I was doing wrong. I was following the directions as best as I could remember, but this Rocco's Pizzas just kept reappearing. Unless they were opening franchises on new corners at the same speed I was driving, I had to admit I was lost.

What made this episode very frustrating was that I was doing everything I knew but kept circling back to the same location. Even a *different* pizza place would have been better, because I would have at least felt I was making some progress, albeit in the wrong direction.

In my work with people experiencing reset moments, I see many making this same journey in their efforts to move towards their preferred future.

They may get a few promotions, enter a new relationship, lose a few kilos, but sooner or later they end up having the same conversation with themselves. They are circling back to that same 'pizza place' in their life.

The only way I could move past that pizza place was to stop and ask for directions. Yes, that took a lot of effort (but even for a man it was achievable). Similarly, the only way we will progress as human beings is to learn to ask the right questions about our life direction.

Part of Sam's journey was to understand that the discomfort she'd been experiencing around change was entirely normal. When her boss resented her success, when those around her shared their doubts about her decision to keep working, and when her colleagues called into question what she had worked hard to implement, like anyone she went down the path of questioning her value. Despite all outward appearances and stories that she created about herself, at the end of the day Sam really wanted to be valued for who she was.

We all want people to understand and accept us. This is oxygen for our souls. The opposite is also true. When people don't acknowledge us for who we are, when they question the very root of understanding we have about ourselves or when they dismiss us, then it feels like the very light of our soul is dimmed.

Of course, the better you know yourself, the harder it is for people to dim your light. One reason our light dims too readily is that either we don't know ourselves well enough or we are trying to live an identity that is not true to ourselves. It has been said that 'We make a great us ... but a lousy other.'

One day I was having a conversation with a client, who was trying to work out how to be accepted by a group of people they felt continually rejected by. There was no business interest in being accepted by these people; rather, it was a personal validation they were seeking. After circling around the topic for a while, I observed that maybe the reason my client couldn't figure out how to be accepted by this group of people was that they had nothing in common. 'Maybe,' I said, 'these people aren't your people.'

My client reacted strongly to this. 'Look, Steve,' they retorted, 'it's an emotional pull. I know that if I am accepted by them, then my life's efforts will have been worthwhile.'

Being the highly empathetic coach that I am, I simply asked, 'What if you get into the group and you realise that you don't actually like them?' Unfortunately, my client was not immediately able to process that as a possible outcome.

Understanding ourselves is more than just feel-good psychology: it goes to the core of who we are as human beings.

If we are truly to reset and recalibrate our lives, we must honestly understand our make-up and live in line with who we have been created to be. This is not a jail sentence, whereby we just accept our lot and therefore stay stagnant, but rather an opportunity to discover the unique being that we are and then leverage this towards achieving our preferred future.

To help us understand who we are and our real value to this world, we need to be able to answer the following questions:

- What gives me the fuel to keep moving forward?
- What guides my decision making?
- How am I wired?

So, let's do some thinking.

What gives me the fuel to keep moving forward? (My purpose)

To truly thrive we need to be fuelled by something greater than our work (paid or otherwise).

Yes, our job is an important part of who we are, and doing our work well definitely can provide a buzz. That buzz, however, will not last forever. While important to our wellbeing, the mere act of working is not sufficient to live a life fuelled by passion.

If we truly are to live a life that will move us into our best future, we need to be fuelled by something deeper. What is it that fuels you to keep going? What gives you the passion to get up in the morning? Essentially: what gives you a sense of meaning?

Every one of us has a yearning for significance; to be something more than a body who clocks in for work in the morning and then out again in the evening. On the other hand, not everyone wants to change the world ... and that is fine! I mean, imagine the chaos that would ensue if that were the case, as we all have very different ideas about the changes the world needs. However, we all want to be valued for who we truly are – this is the deep cry of every human heart. What that looks and feels like is unique to every individual.

Achieving world peace is not the ambition of every person who walks this planet. There are those people who see global possibilities, the number of people they can impact and the world that could be. While this is a noble pursuit, it is not for everyone. The desire to make a meaningful contribution to the lives of your children, to see a small group of students achieve more than they thought possible, or to help the local football club run smoothly are all equally noble pursuits.

I have been inspired by a whole range of different life meanings: from those who are fuelled by a purpose to create physically and emotionally healthy families; those who want to make the community they live in a more welcoming place; those who dedicate their lives to running smooth operating systems; those with wealth who are philanthropy-minded; and, very importantly, those who are all about creating great coffee experiences.

A question I like to ask my clients (and those people unfortunate enough to be cornered by me at a party) is: 'What is it that keeps you going?'

Now, I don't mean wine or coffee or the need to see your footy team win. More seriously, I mean what keeps you going when work gets tough or boring, when family becomes difficult or when life seems to be conspiring against you? The answer will be the fuel that keeps you going.

The act of making coffee is not a purpose – it is a task. The desire to provide a relaxed vibe where people can connect, chill out and enjoy quality coffee will, however, keep the coffee shop owner going through the tough times and long hours if that is their underlying purpose in owning a coffee shop. The desire to have a trendy coffee shop with good coffee and nothing deeper will mean that when things get tough, the owners will probably walk away. The desire to run a successful business rarely provides the fuel a person needs during tough times and long nights, but the dream of providing a legacy or meeting a specific need will.

A purpose that is greater than just myself will keep me motivated and focused when things get difficult. The desire to unlock potential and witness people functioning at their best is what keeps me going during those hectic times when I struggle to keep up. At the end of the day, the sacrifices I make are not generated by a need to make more money, give great presentations or meet interesting people; instead, I am driven by the joy of helping people realise their potential. We all need this kind of deeper reason for doing what we do – it can be described as our 'moral purpose', if you like.

What guides my decision making? (My values)

Time is a limited resource and we are all allocated the same amount. No matter how wise or frugal we are with its expenditure, there are only 168 hours per week. No matter what I do at the end of that 168th hour, the next week starts – I cannot stop it no matter how much I wish I could. There are only 168 hours, 10,080 minutes, 604,800 seconds a week, nothing more, nothing less!

The reality of this is a bit like my suitcase: there is a finite amount I can fit in ... no amount of stuffing, sitting on it or cursing will shift that capacity (though my wife is always trying to test the limits of this reality). I need to learn to work within the limits (and yes, that was hard for me to say).

In case you are wondering, this is not an obligatory section on time management. Yes, time management is a useful skill; as is the concept of working smarter, not harder. However, these concepts, while appearing to be useful, can in fact be derailers. No matter how often I hear these phrases, at some point I reach capacity all over again. My calendar is packed full, with no seconds lost ... and yet some significant priorities always seem to have missed being added.

> Our personal values are what is important to us in life. They are the 'roots' that go far deeper than our personality, and they are the lens through which we evaluate everything.

At this point it is always important for me to go back to those few guiding principles I try to live my life by. These principles allow me to determine who I accept work from, who I make time for and how I choose to allocate any remaining time.

I have a default position that always leaves me wanting to do a lot more than I have the time capacity for. I then end up being very frustrated by not being able to do everything. When I was younger, that was when the dummy spits would start. It seems my dad was right when he told me: 'Steve, you need to focus on a few things rather than trying to do everything or be everything for all people.' (Yes, Dad, you heard me correctly ... you were r ... r ... r ... r ... right ...)

The guiding principles keep me focused on what I allocate my time to, and from this I can tell what my priorities are. These guiding principles – and therefore my priorities – are driven by my personal values and influenced by my life goals.

Our personal values are what is important to us in life. They are the 'roots' that go far deeper than our personality, and they are the lens through which we evaluate everything.

A number of years ago, social psychologist and researcher Professor Shalom Schwartz found that there are ten personal values that are common across all cultures. They are:

- Conformity
- Tradition
- Security
- Power
- Achievement
- Hedonism
- Stimulation
- Self-direction
- Universalism
- Benevolence.

It may seem hard to believe that there are only ten values, but once you unpack what they are, they form a useful framework for understanding our deepest core drivers. I won't go into this further here, but would encourage you to check out www.personalvaluesgames.com to discover your own.

Figuring out my own guiding principles

While I was working on this section, I was wrestling with how much time I needed to allocate to my client-coaching business compared with my writing, as well as the amount of time I needed to give to be a fully present husband, catch up with friends and connect with my family. And I also needed to find some time for myself. I was so busy with the business, due to unexpected growth, that it created unprecedented demands on my time and resources. While I counted myself incredibly blessed to be in this position during a global pandemic, it seemed that every new opportunity took me away from the other parts of my life I wanted to develop and focus on.

The goal of trying to prioritise my time meant that work always won out, as there was always a new idea, new client or a presentation to deliver. Plus, I was hiring new team members and new employees. Due to my high standards (or inability to let go and trust others), my time was quickly eroded. Understanding my personal values of achievement (being competent and driving for success), self-direction (mastery over my own life direction) and stimulation (the need for variety and adventure) helped me to reflect accurately that unless something within me changed, work was always going to dominate.

My relationships, writing, study and time for myself were also important, and unless I changed my motivations, nothing else would change.

I had to get tough!

I knew from experience that adhering to a simple time-allocation plan would probably not work. Although I am very disciplined and organised when it comes to allocating my time, it would not sustain me when it mattered. So I needed to re-evaluate my guiding principles and come up with strong psychological drivers that would motivate and change my behaviour.

My first reflection was that I desired to be a thought-leader and influencer, and therefore needed to allocate energy to these pursuits. The second involved the 'why' behind my desire to write and speak publicly. I wished to help others from a position of strength, deep knowledge and expertise. To do so meant I needed to write, to pursue learning, if I truly wanted to provide expertise. Remember, these are my personal values and drivers and may not resonate with you at all (and that's okay – they work for me).

I also desired to spend more time with my wife and family (whether they wanted it or not). To some people this might seem like a ridiculous thought ... if my family were so important, then of course I would spend time with them! I understand that for a lot of people it is that simple; unfortunately, for me the desire often does not follow practice, as I become too busy working on new ideas with great clients. A downside of my personal values is I tend to get very caught up in the exciting work I do and forget about other important people.

At the end of my life, it will be my family who will stand around me. Again, knowing all of this was not enough. I needed to articulate a principle that would sustain me spending time with them even when business opportunities arose. My principle became: 'Time invested now will reap dividends into the future.' Again, this may or may not resonate with you, but that's okay because it is my principle, not yours. There is no right or wrong with developing and articulating principles, they just need to resonate and ring true for you. They must be personal and have meaning for you!

Of course, principles without actions attached are useless. They are merely puffs of hot air that sound good but lead nowhere. This is where the power of habits comes into play (more on that later). This statement below emerged from my personal values. It is the motivation behind what I do, how I live my life and what drives me.

Steve's guiding principles

My work as a consulting organisational psychologist, entrepreneur, husband, father, eldest sibling, favourite child (that was just to check if any of my siblings read this) is an integral part of what makes me who I am. It is, however, an outworking of my identity rather than being at the core of who I am. My relationships, family of origin, vocation choices, sporting teams I follow, talents and the like are all important, but they don't answer the deep question of who I am.

Being a fantastic husband (okay, this might be an ambition rather than reality) is a key part of who I am, but who I am at my core defines how I go about being a partner to the one I love. The way I interact with my wife reflects what I truly value. In my pursuit to be a better partner I need to reflect on how this is working and whether I am happy with what is coming out.

> At my core is a person who is defined by a desire for people I interact with to thrive. I am defined by the desire to have a significant impact on people. I hold the belief that while I cannot change anyone, I can set up an environment where people are challenged, reflective and motivated to be all that they can be.

I asked Sam to reflect on her values using the ten common values as set out by Professor Schwartz and then write her guiding principles. This is what she came up with:

Sam loves life and loves people. She needs to be in right relationship with those closest to her in work and play. When this balance is not met then Sam works hard to restore the relationship and, if this is not possible, she will move on from them. Sam is not responsible for others' happiness but will always live life in a way that seeks to meet the needs of those in her circle.

As Sam reflected on her values of benevolence (caring for those in her circle) and conformity (wanting to maintain harmony), she realised why she was stuck in a loop of people-pleasing. Even though she had acknowledged this earlier, the defining of her personal values allowed her to deeply understand why she kept circling back to the same default behaviours. It was truly a game changer for her.

How am I wired? (My personality)

One of my favourite places in the world to spend with my wife relaxing, writing, contemplating, reflecting and drinking wine is in the south-west of the state in which I live. Surrounded by the sea, bush and great wineries, I find there is not a better place to be. Sometimes, when driving to our destination, I pose a very deep question to whoever will listen. It is usually something like: 'I wonder what it is like to be a cow?' My wife often stares at me with that look that says she struggles to understand why anyone would pay me for advice and, occasionally, voices her concern for my mental health.

> When we can understand our personal values and how they shape our personality, then we are able to more accurately reflect on and ask questions about how we are wired.

I know it's a bizarre question, but I *do* often wonder whether cows get cold or hot, bored of grass, annoyed by the cars zooming by, or whether they have any consciousness, dreams or ambitions. Now, I don't mean to start an existential debate and I know the question is silly, but I sometimes think the same question when observing people. No, I don't wonder what it's like for them to be a cow, but I am fascinated by what it is like to be them.

You see, I only have one lens on life and that is mine. Of course, I can walk in other people's shoes and empathise with them, but I am still doing that from my point of view. Even the most aware among us are still observing and interacting with others from our own point of reference.

What this all boils down to is that I am really curious about other people's innate wiring or personality.

Our personality provides us with a unique toolkit with which we engage with our world, and it is how we make decisions about how we will respond. While this sounds systematic, it is really an unconscious process. Just as a cow is a cow and doesn't have much choice about that, our personality influences every part of us whether we like it or not.

We do, however, have some control over how we understand our personality and how we leverage our uniqueness, and this is what I want to explore. When we can understand our personal values and how they shape our personality, then we are able to more accurately reflect on and ask questions about how we are wired.

When coaching or working with groups of people, one of the first exercises I ask them to do is explore their values and personality. This is not for my own curiosity but because it helps explain so much about the individual or group. A family I was working with had three adult children who were extroverted and very gregarious. However, Dad was introverted and a deep thinker. He was frustrated that whenever he wanted to engage his children in financial legacy conversations they would muck around, invite friends over and be up and down to the kitchen all the time. They all took a values and personality questionnaire and it quickly became obvious what was going on.

Dad's thinking style was to take on all the information, process it internally and then test the ideas he wanted to explore through debate. His children loved to think out loud, test their ideas with friends and be active as they chatted. While his intentions were great, he was not speaking his kids' language and was just getting frustrated. In fact, everyone was getting frustrated with everyone. Once we understood the different interaction styles, we explored how everyone's needs could be met and, happily, this family went on to have great family meetings.

Some of you reading this may have already completed a number of personality questionnaires and assessments, while others of you may never have explored these tools. I will focus on both situations. From experiences like the one described with the family above, I believe that being aware of your personality provides you with deep insight about yourself and an understanding of why you may keep circling back to the same place in your personal life – and in your work life, which I will cover in the section below.

Seeing the value in your personality assessment

Like my client Sam, some of you have probably completed these assessments either as part of your self-development programs or in your place of employment.

From the number of conversations I have had with corporate leaders over the years, I generally hear the comment that 'while the tests were useful in informing me about myself they just reconfirm the same things'. Within this group of people there often appears to be a reluctance to change, or almost a belief that the positive and negative traits described in the test results are set in stone. While they are aware of their traits, there is not a whole lot they can do to change them.

One of the criticisms of focusing on personality traits is that it tends to drive an egocentric view of the world. It often plays out through statements such as: 'This is who I am, so now others need to learn to engage with me.'

A good understanding of personality traits provides the user with not only an understanding of their own strengths but also the strengths of those around them. This deeper knowledge provides individuals with a true understanding of others and an appreciation for the strengths others can bring. Rather than expecting others to engage with the world through their own lens, they can fully appreciate the complementary strengths of other people and allow them to shine. It allows people to work together in ways that suit them all.

A good understanding of personality traits provides the user with not only an understanding of their own strengths but also the strengths of those around them.

A deeper understanding of your personality means you also become more aware of both your positive and negative traits. As human beings we all have positive strengths and characteristics, but we also have another side to us. This is referred by psychologists as our shadow (or dark) side.

This phrase was first coined by Swiss psychiatrist and psychoanalyst Carl Jung. It refers to those aspects of our personality that we choose to repress or neglect and which, as a consequence, can derail us and/or negatively impact those around us.

One example of 'darker' personality traits includes someone being so emotional that other people become unsettled. This type of person also tends to act quickly and takes risks to 'move the ball down the field', but may at times leave those around them gasping for breath or wondering if they have any self-discipline. Such a person is able to focus on the details to ensure a high level of excellence, but often leaves others feeling they can never meet their exacting demands. They can have a strong drive to create safety for themselves and those around them, but they may not take up new opportunities out of fear.

Having said that, each of these attributes can be important in living your dream life – and in running a successful business. But as indicated above, they have a dark side that can play out in the workplace as much as in everyday life. People who are emotionally expressive can leave an office full of colleagues walking on eggshells. Coworkers may not speak up for fear of an outburst or may choose not to use their initiative because they aren't sure where they stand. Leaders who display this amount of emotional colour inadvertently create a toxic culture, where they can be accused of bullying and/or constantly shifting the goalposts of expectation.

If someone is unaware of this dark side, they may keep arriving at the same place in their leadership. Even if they *are* aware of their darker tendencies, they often lack strategies to change their impact on the workplace.

Awareness of this potential dark side provides a development option. Part of the person's journey at this point may well be to further understand their personality impact, including dark-side tendencies, and develop a plan for managing this part of who they are. Often this requires the use of robust psychometrics and coaching.

Before you can be a leader of others, you need to know clearly who you are and what your core values are. Once you know that, then you can give those values a voice and feel comfortable sharing them with others

I am sometimes asked whether it is worth changing, given the success an individual has achieved to this point. My response is always to ask whether the person is happy with where they are. If they are, then at some level it can be argued that change may not be necessary.

However, if you wish to recalibrate your life, it becomes an important part of the process. Understanding who you are (regardless of your success to this point) provides an opportunity to get to know yourself more deeply and then decide if a recalibration is needed in order to be a better version of yourself. At the end of the day, only you can decide if that is what you want to do.

Before you can be a leader of others, you need to know clearly who you are and what your core values are. Then you can give those values a voice ...

A personality assessment framework

This whole personality journey may be relatively new to you. (Of course, it is not that new from a life standpoint, as you have always had one. If you don't have a personality, then this book may not be for you.) Joking aside, while we all have our unique personalities, we may not have the language or framework to understand what drives us, how our lens differs from others, or how our personality can explain a lot about who we are.

I want to use a simple but effective framework for understanding yourself. Think about the preferences you have for the following four areas of your life:

- Where you get your energy from.
- How you like to take in information.
- The way you make decisions.
- How you prefer to live your life.

(A website such as www.16personalities.com is a great free way to kickstart this journey.)

For those wanting a quick overview, here are four questions – based on the Myers-Briggs Type Indicator test – that will offer a simple way to understand your preferences for how you like to live your life.

Where do your get your energy? Some of us like to process our thinking out loud and get our energy from being around people (i.e. extroverts). Sure, we need some time on our own, but when we are around people we find ourselves feeling energised. Others like to process their thinking before speaking and need alone time to re-energise (i.e. introverts). Understanding where we get our energy is important. If I like to think out loud and receive energy from those around me, then people will be an important part of my world. As someone once said about being an extrovert: 'I'll know what I think when I hear myself talk.' Likewise, if you need to process internally before speaking or making up your mind, then you need to make sure you allow yourself space and not be pressured into being vocal all the time.

How do you like to get the story? How do you like to receive new information? There are some who like to get the full picture by understanding all the different pieces first (i.e. sensing), while others think of an idea and then find the pieces that help them understand that picture (i.e. intuition). There are those who speak in concrete language, use specific examples and like to hear the facts. There are others who tend to speak more in the abstract and be a bit vague at times. In the case of those who like to make sure the detail is correct, you are probably more of a sensor (i.e. using your senses to understand the world). If you are more intuitive in understanding information, then you are what we call an intuitive.

How do you arrive at decisions? When making decisions, some lead with their heart (feeling) and others lead with their head (thinking). It's not that one type of person cares more than the other; rather, the difference lies in what drives their decision making. If you are someone who has a process for making decisions, then you are a thinker. If you tend to make decisions based on how they will impact other people, then you are what we call a feeler. Thinkers tend to try to find a process that works for the most amount of people in the majority of scenarios, whereas the feeler processes each decision based on its perceived impact on different individuals.

How do you like to live your life? Do you like to have your life organised and structured (i.e. a judging approach) or do you leave your options open because you don't want to be pinned down (i.e. a perceiving approach)? It's not that judgers can't be spontaneous or that perceivers are unorganised, it's just our preference for how we like to live life. If you find yourself leaving things to the last minute or if your best work seems to emerge just before the deadline, then it is highly probable you are a perceiver. If you find yourself planning for times to be spontaneous, then you are more likely to be a judger.

If this style of personality assessment is not for you, or if you would like to investigate this area more fully, then I suggest you look at a great book by David Keirsey called *Please Understand Me II*.

So why does this all matter?

Personality preferences are not about putting you in a box with no room to move. Rather, they are about helping us understand our preferences for how we approach life. I could learn to write with my left hand, but it would take more energy and would never be quite as effective as using my right hand. Our personality preferences are a bit the same. Extroverts can process their thinking internally, but when under stress they will want to 'talk it out'. The energy it requires to be something else may be robbing the world of our value and tiring us out.

Once we understand our personality preferences, we can begin to understand who we are. We can then start to identify whether we are chasing goals that may be the antithesis of our true selves, or which are not aligned with the way we naturally see the world.

Your inner world: exploring your spiritual self

After we had explored her personal values and personality traits, I looked at Sam and told her: 'Now it's time to get spiritual.'

She smiled at me nervously. 'Wow, this process just keeps surprising me.'

'I think it is really important to look at what fuels you,' I replied. 'What keeps you going when work gets tough, when family becomes difficult or when life seems to be conspiring against you? What is truly important to you? What causes you stress? What are your default behaviours when you are stressed? When do you truly shine? What are you doing? Where are you? Who are you with? What are you focused on?'

Some people are fuelled by setting up the family and the next generation; others by writing the next great novel; and others still by creating gifts or moments that bring a smile to someone's face. These all refer to a purpose outside of oneself, and this can be thought of as the spiritual dimension. Our 'why' in life is very related to our spiritual self.

Sam smiled and said, 'Oh, this is a conversation I am comfortable with. I had just never thought it would be part of this discussion.'

I believe that we are spiritual beings designed to connect with a higher power; something that is greater than ourselves and beyond our normal existence. Your spiritual connection will provide the fuel you need to thrive. It is also a vital component of our overall health and wellbeing.

If we don't take the time to connect with our spiritual side, it is like owning a Stradivarius violin but not playing it. A Stradivarius violin is made to create music, not just sit inside its case. In the hands of a skilled musician, it sings beautiful notes. We are all made to 'sing', to shine, to truly live. This only really happens if we embrace who we are and get in touch with the higher purpose that drives our values. People who have no connection with their spiritual connection never truly sing ... they merely exist.

Sam's sense of spiritual self rested strongly in her connection to nature. She felt that she was a connected part of a whole and that every action had repercussions throughout the universe. She felt connected to the universe and, because of that, felt the pain when the universe was out of sync. Her guiding philosophies were:

- The universe is protecting life.
- All people are connected to the universe and therefore need to be treated as such.
- Life is precious and infinite.
- Pain has purpose, and I need to accept this as a gift and discover what the purpose might be.

My spiritual self comes from a deep faith in God. It may be different for you, and that is your choice; however, I would encourage you to contemplate your spiritual self and how it impacts your guiding philosophies. My spiritual self has led me to the following guiding philosophies:

- Everyone has been created by God to live a great life.
- All people deserve to be treated with dignity.
- No one person has all the truth, and I need to stay in a listening pose.
- Life is to be lived in service of others.
- This world was created beautifully and is for us to enjoy and curate.

I have worked with people who are devout Hindus, with those who worship Allah, and with others who follow the spirits of their ancestors, or live in harmony with their chakras, and more ... there are so many different ways of engaging with something outside of ourselves. When people are connected to their spiritual side, I have noticed they have a far greater ability to live according to their guiding principles.

The University of Minnesota has put together a great resource called *Develop Your Spiritual Resources*, which provides a range of activities, experiences and tools that will help you understand spirituality, and your spiritual self, in more detail.

Reviewing what makes you, you

Take some time to ponder the following questions in order to discover your own internal wiring.

- What were your top three values? (www.personalvaluesgames.com)
- How did the Myers Briggs categories (www.16personalities.com) describe you, and did those descriptions resonate? (It's okay to go and do some research to understand these categories in more detail if you wish.)
- What guides your decision making? (i.e. what spiritual component is important to you?)

Based on your answers, what do your guiding principles need to be for this next period of your life?

LET'S RECAP:

What are my strengths?

- Our life's meaning and purpose are inseparably linked to our identity. The closer we can live in alignment with our identity, the more likely we are to live a fulfilled life.
- Taking time to reflect on our identity helps us understand our unique purpose and way of fulfilling it.
- Once we are clear about our personal values, we tend to make decisions that are more aligned with our identity and that will sustain us in life.
- Living in a manner that is congruent with the way we are wired up is far less stressful and takes a lot less effort than the alternative.
- The fuel that keeps us going through the transition is often found within our spiritual self.

Reset

Review

Reaquaint

Recalibrate

Recalibrate: *'To shift the way you think and act in order to achieve your desired outcome.' This final step provides the tools for setting yourself up for success. By reflecting on what you want, you can begin to recalibrate your life and move in the direction of your preferred future.*

What am I prepared to give up?

Sam and I were now quite a few sessions into her journey of self-discovery. It was clear that Sam was beginning to enjoy the process. However, it was time now for the rubber to hit the road, so to speak. Was Sam actually prepared to start to put a plan to change into action?

Helping someone unlock their own deep drivers for change provides insight into how successful they will be. If the change is a vague idea that life could be better, then such a mindset rarely sustains effort.

We must not only have a desire for change, we need to have thought about what the change really entails.

In other words: what am I prepared to give up? This is the fourth key question as you make your transition.

The reality is, we know people maintain unhelpful behaviours because they have been receiving, consciously or unconsciously, some reward from it. Some of us may eat too much, but the reward is tasty food and short-lived satisfaction. Other people continually end up in unhealthy relationships, but then their friends spend time commiserating about those relationships with them and giving them attention. I could go on, but the simple truth is that these subconscious rewards are powerful drivers.

> Helping someone unlock their own deep drivers for change provides insight into how successful they will be. If the change is a vague idea that life could be better, then such a mindset rarely sustains effort.

As I explored this with Sam, I explained that to bring about the change she was looking for she would need to have a vision of what could be – or, in other words, her preferred future. She needed to believe that she could successfully make the change. Sam also had to believe that she had the resources at her disposal to enact the change.

I explained that discipline was required, but discipline was actually the easy part. Yes, you heard right! If I understand what it is I am trying to change and have truly bought into the image of the future I am moving towards, then I will already have the most important element in place.

Developing new habits to enable change

Of course, Sam needed a plan. One that involved her putting in place achievable behaviours (we call these habits) that would move her towards the change. These habits would help shift those strong existing neural pathways and beliefs, and create and strengthen new ones that would, in turn, create and sustain change.

Sustaining new habits over a period of time will bring a new equilibrium. Sam had been in a state that was comfortable (though not preferable) for a long time, so shifting would require a concerted effort. That's why sticking at these habits for longer than you think necessary is important to truly embed behaviours.

After experiencing a tumultuous life event or going through a period of reflection where we have realised things probably need to be different, making the changes that need to be made is not always an appealing prospect. In reality, we often wish we could just continue to do what we have been doing and have life turn out the way we hope it will ... without any real effort on our part.

Unfortunately, life rarely works like that. (I am still looking for that magic pill myself, by the way.) I saw a great cartoon once that depicted two shop counters, each one intended for people seeking life change. The line of people queuing for the counter with 'Pills and Potions' went out the door – but the line for the 'Doing things differently' counter was empty.

A successful transition is not about trying to turn our lives upside down. Rather, it is about shifting our thinking and behaviours to be more aligned with where we are going.

Have you ever decided that you are going to run a marathon to get fit, connect up with old friends to rebuild relationships, do everything the boss says to get ahead at work, or eat a lot more green vegetables so you are the healthiest version of you?

The problem with each of these approaches is that unless you have been running for a while, connecting with a few friends regularly, eating reasonably healthily or working in line with your boss's ideals, enacting change becomes almost overwhelming. You haven't developed the foundational behaviours that will allow you to reach out and live your goals. It's more than a matter of willpower.

We are going to chat about willpower a little later, and it's important to note that while it is our friend, it is also not a friend without limits. You may be able to stick at your new habits for a while, but most people eventually slip back into old behaviours. The amount of effort needed to sustain the new way forward is too great, and so we have set ourselves up to fail, even though we started with great intent.

I would like to suggest that the more effective long-term solution is to focus on recalibrating your life ... slightly. As each new habit is established, you can think about expanding it or adding a new one. As you continue to do this, a new normal is created and then you recalibrate from that level. Over time you are running marathons, maintaining quality relationships, being more engaged at work and drinking only green smoothies (okay, that last one may be a step too far).

I know that doesn't sound as sexy as 'Change your life in two easy steps' or 'Be your perfect self in five weeks', but it is ultimately a plan that will work long term.

Let's chat about what it might take to really enable ourselves to change.

> A successful transition is not about trying to turn our lives upside down. Rather, it is about shifting our thinking and behaviours to be more aligned with where we are going.

There is an old story I remember reading about how to catch a monkey. I am no animal expert and so I have no way of validating this but ... the story goes that if you wish to catch a monkey you put a bunch of peanuts into a bottle with an opening just big enough for the monkey to slip its open hand into. When the monkey grabs the peanuts and tries to remove its hand, the opening is not big enough for the monkey's hand and peanuts to exit the bottle.

Of course, because the monkey wants the peanuts it won't let go of them. And *voilà,* you have the monkey captured. (Again, not sure why you would want to capture a monkey or even if that approach is valid ... and I am not suggesting we all go out and test the validity of the story on animals or small children!).

The point of the story is that at any time the monkey can escape. All it must do is let go of the peanuts and its hand will be able to exit the top of the bottle. However, as it is not prepared to do that, there is no way for the monkey to escape.

I wonder what you are holding onto that you are not prepared to let go and that is keeping you trapped?

Changing behaviour is one of the more difficult tasks any of us can undertake. And you thought cage-diving with sharks or jumping out of a plane with some form of parachute were tough gigs? If sheer willpower was enough, we would all be living our preferred futures now. The problem with willpower is that it is not a strong enough driver of change by itself.

Don't get me wrong – it *is* important. Research by psychologist Roy Baumeister shows that self-control is essential to changing habits. But in their book *Willpower: Why Self-Control is the Secret of Success*, Roy Baumeister and his co-author John Tierney point to research demonstrating that while willpower is essential, it is also a finite resource.

In a well-known experiment, since replicated a number of times in a variety of ways, Baumeister showed that when you have to use willpower, your decision-making about other things becomes depleted. In the experiment called The Chocolate and Radish Experiment, a group of people were asked to sit in a room where chocolate chip biscuits had just been baked. You can just imagine the smell in that room! On the table in front of them was a bowl of those biscuits and a bowl of radishes. Half the group were told that they could only eat from the bowl of radishes, whereas the other half were allowed to eat both the radishes and the biscuits. Then both groups were given an unsolvable geometric-based puzzle to complete (don't you just love psychologists?). What they found was that the group who had been only allowed to eat the radishes persisted with the test for a shorter period of time before giving up. Resisting the chocolate biscuits had depleted their ability to persevere, as compared to the other half of the group who spent much longer trying to complete the test.

It sounds simplistic, but this was an indicator that our willpower is a finite resource. As mentioned, countless experiments have since shown the same phenomenon. Why is this important? It means that we need to decide *where* we are going to use our willpower, otherwise we will find ourselves trying to use it for *all* our behaviour changes and failing miserably (sound familiar?)

Identifying our deep underlying beliefs

If willpower by itself is not enough to enable change, what can? If good intentions and hard work were sufficient, we would be living our preferred lives now. The reality is that despite the motivation and intent to change, we often find ourselves back at step one.

Why is this the case?

Being a typical psychologist, I will answer this question with another question. (You are welcome.) After talking this through with Sam, I told her that now it was time for the most important question of all:

'What is it that you are prepared to give up in order to change, and what are you not prepared to give up?'

Sam looked out the window and sat silently for a while. In fact, she was silent for so long I also looked out the window to see what had grabbed her attention.

'I don't know,' she finally said. 'I like everything in my life, but at the same time I don't like the way my life is.'

I smiled. 'That's why I'm here. The key to change lies in unpacking the deeper reasons behind those things you are willing to change and those you are not.'

One of the reasons we don't change is that we have strong underlying beliefs which have cemented themselves in our psyche without us realising it. They may have arisen from our upbringing, from information we received that deeply resonated with us (even if it wasn't accurate), or from experiences that have reinforced certain ways of thinking.

In this case, we are a bit like the monkey with a fistful of peanuts. Struggling to escape but unwilling to give up certain beliefs.

It is important to acknowledge that there is no one correct response to the question I posed to Sam.

We all have deep beliefs that we hold onto tightly. Scotch is one of mine (and yes, I am referring to a quality single malt), a good quality red is another. On a more serious note, autonomy in my work is something I am not prepared to give up. I understand this precludes me from certain roles that I have been approached to do. Provided I am honest with myself about it, this is okay.

It is when I am not prepared to give up something but in the same breath complain that I am hamstrung, that I am not being honest about the desire to change.

Life is about choices. We all make them on a small scale and a large scale. The tension emerges when we refuse to acknowledge those things we won't give up and yet expect to have different results.

For example, a statement I have heard from several clients is: 'I want to change my work, but I am not prepared to give up my current standard of income.' I point out to them that acknowledging this is not a problem. They must, however, appreciate that what they are actually saying is: 'I will only change if I am remunerated enough.' The reality is if that if they do leave their current job they will probably end up in a similar one because the dollars are a strong driver. This may be because they have a lot of outgoings and responsibilities (at least, it will be rationalised this way) but it probably points to a deeper driver. Again, this is not a right or wrong situation.

> It is when I am not prepared to give up something but in the same breath complain that I am hamstrung, that I am not being honest about the desire to change.

Toni was a young entrepreneur when I first met them. They had a dream for developing an ethical approach to investing. Through some great connections and lots of hard work, they built a successful business. The business grew so quickly that a larger investment house approached them to acquire the whole company. Toni was conflicted. It would be a great financial return and would elevate them to a different sphere of wealth. But Toni knew that as part of the purchase they would need to stay involved in the business for a few years and that their love for ethical investing was not a strong driver for the purchasing firm. Friends had told Toni that as they were only 30 years old, why care if they did five years with the investor? Toni would make loads of money, set themselves up and in five years could start something else. Toni made the decision to sell.

Toni came to me two years after the sale, clearly unhappy. They were out of alignment with their values but had purchased a house that they would not be able to afford if they left before the five-year period was up. Toni had assets and could start over again, but felt that if they gave up this job their standard of living would drop and their partner would need to go back to work.

Of course, this is a tough position to be in.

We worked through the process and ultimately Toni felt that the financial reward was too great for them to leave. They then had to conclude that this was their life for the next few years, and so our sessions became about how to live well within these less-than-ideal constraints.

While this may not have been an ideal outcome, it was one Toni was honest about – and so they were able to design their life in such a way that they could still live well in all regards. They realised through the work we did together that financial security for them and their family was of the highest importance. This was driven by personal values, as well as by many life experiences.

Avoiding arrogance: unleashing our best life

Acknowledging what you are prepared to give up is never easy and rarely a one-time decision.

Although we are sometimes unaware of our non-negotiables until we think through them, there may also be some deep reasons behind them. It is worth acknowledging that sometimes we may have a reasonably superficial reason for not giving something up (like me and my Scotch or wine), and that's okay, as long as we are honest about it and the constraints it may put on us.

I remember being a very reasonable person as a teenager. I had well-thought-out plans, my opinions were very mature, and I could not believe that so much stupidity existed in the world. I mean, how could people with so much talked-about experience not understand my clever ways? Why would they insist on me being in bed by certain times, helping around the house with menial tasks, and attending family functions? I reached the conclusion that my parents were clearly out of touch with reality and I would parent very differently if I ever had the chance.

Fast forward a few years and here I am having the 'no you can't go to that party' conversation with my stepson and finding myself using the well-worn parenting phrase: 'because we are your parents and we know what's best'. Any parent who has had this conversation knows exactly how it ends ... yelling, slammed doors and lots of anger (and my son wasn't much better, either).

Like any other teenager, I knew best from my limited experience. Turns out there was much I didn't know but would learn later in life. However, as a parent I was guilty of committing the same error. It wasn't that I wanted to protect my son or wanted the best for him. It was the error of not really listening and arrogantly thinking that by simply saying 'because I told you so' he would understand my point of view. Yes, I did use the word arrogance.

Arrogance is an attitude and behaviour that declares, 'I know best and I don't need to listen to you.' Arrogance positions you as the holder of truth and others as needing your wisdom. Arrogance looks like that person who you try to have a conversation with but all they want to do is defend their point of view. Arrogance is being right all the time. I mean, think about it, can anyone be right all the time? Arrogance blocks us from living our best life.

In his book *Conscious Business,* executive coach and business advisor Fred Kofman explains this concept in a manner that is confronting but also helpful. He describes arrogance as a 'knower mindset.' This is the mindset of a person who knows everything, who knows that they are right, who knows that if they just keep speaking you will eventually come around to their way of thinking. If we are honest with ourselves, we can all fall into this mindset. When we are emotionally involved in something, have a lot of expertise, are tired, stressed or very comfortable with the topic, we can find ourselves displaying this kind of arrogance.

'I already know why this is not working.'

'They just need to change and then I will be able to ...'

'I just need to work harder.'

'I just need to find the right man.'

'I just haven't found the right job that truly allows me to shine.'

The problem with having such a mindset is that we are truly not seeking to understand. We may have a lot of previous experience, expertise and plain old stubbornness that enables us to justify our position and closed-off way of thinking. The simple and confronting truth is that when we are in such a mindset we will never truly move forward or take advantage of the opportunity a life transition offers us.

A knower often spends little time reflecting. Knowers surround themselves with people who will pat them on the back and remind them how 'right' they are. Knowers like these kinds of people because they don't challenge the status quo or provide confronting alternate views.

Fred Kofman also highlights the opposite kind of mindset that we can all strive to practise, that of a 'learner'.

A person with a learner mindset will seek to understand another's point of view, trying to walk in someone else's shoes and not just pay lip service to 'understanding' other people. Having a learner mindset says that while I know a lot and have expertise, I am always interested in exploring new ideas and different ways of doing things. A learner mindset keeps you open to the world and new ways of doing.

Having a learner mindset requires a certain level of humility and an ability to stay open to the fact that others may have a better way of doing or being. Learners often ask themselves (and others) 'What if?' questions: 'What if there is another way?' What if I was wrong?' 'What if I changed what I know?'

Learners also ask themselves 'Why?' questions. 'Why is what I know not working?' 'Why do I keep getting the same results?'

A learner recognises that life often doesn't dish up simple answers and that there is not a 'right' answer, only 'best' answers to some of life's biggest issues (and some of the small ones, like why I don't ever shut the kitchen cupboards). Okay, that last one was about me trying to rationalise why, after all these years of marriage, I still forget to shut doors.

A learner is self-aware and understands that we all have both strengths and limitations. They understand that perfection is not possible as a human being and therefore some of the attributes they most value may, in fact, be faulty. Learners are self-reflective and prepared to change as the evidence changes in front of them.

A word of caution

Before you instinctively throw all knowers under the bus, remember that most of us fluctuate between the two states.

While I strive hard to be open minded, reflective and embrace new ways of doing things, I can easily become defensive when my way is challenged.

How, then, do I try and stay in the learner mindset? Here are a couple of suggestions:

- Be aware of my defensiveness. Being in tune with when I become defensive is a great tool to have. We often become defensive when our deeply held assumptions or beliefs are challenged. Being aware of when we become defensive is the first step to recognising when we are probably about to entrench ourselves into knower territory.
- Get into the habit of asking questions where you don't already know the answers. Questions asked with the intent of truly understanding, rather than to look for answers that confirm our position.

- Deliberately engage with people and experiences that provide a different view of the world than your own.
- Focus on your own mindset rather than that of those around you.

A learner questions their assumptions about how life works. These assumptions are our mental models, the lens through which we see the world. They will be strongly influenced by our values and worldviews, our personality and our experience (which is why Key Question 3: 'What are my strengths?', page 61, is so important).

What are you prepared to walk away from?

After exploring the conversation about what Sam was prepared and not prepared to give up, it became very clear that she was not prepared to give up her financial income and the status associated with her role. This put her in the situation where she felt she needed to stay in her current job – ironically, the very same one where she had already admitted she was no longer comfortable. I could feel us reaching a bit of a stalemate and I felt that a gentle challenge was needed.

I put it to her: 'Are you prepared to give up those beliefs and corresponding behaviours that might not be helping you embrace this transition opportunity?'

For example, if the belief that you must always put others first is a non-negotiable, then maybe you need to be honest with yourself that you probably will never carve time out to exercise. Instead, maybe you can start to think of ways you can fit exercise in while also putting others first (for example, you could take a walk as a family, or participate in more active family time).

I said to Sam: 'I am not saying this is easy, but it is not until we give up what is holding us back, that we can move forward. Many of us are like that monkey with a fistful of peanuts, wishing that life was different. Until we let go of the peanuts, life will be the same! In my case, I know I must drink less to lose weight, otherwise it's not really going to happen ... despite what we see on TV.

'It is important to be honest with yourself. If you go through this process and decide the benefits of your new future are not worth the effort, then be honest about it. Sure, excessive drinking may lead to an early death, but if you are honest with yourself that you like wine too much to cut back, then that is your decision.

'We cause ourselves mental health stress when we pretend to want to pursue a future that, essentially, we have decided at a deeper level is not for us. Remember, we do what we do because we get some reward for it. If giving up this reward is not compelling enough, we won't change.'

I finished the session by leaving Sam one question to ponder before we next met.

It's a tough one and I leave you with the same:

What beliefs are you prepared to give up and walk away from?

As Steven Furtick, author of *Greater*, describes it, there is always a price to pay to when making a change. Some people like the comfort of being good at something, but to improve or change you need to be prepared to make a sacrifice of some kind – and to not just understand that in theory, but be prepared to put it into action.

How to challenge your assumptions

Author Pamela Meyer, in her book *Leadership Agility*, discusses the importance of regularly challenging assumptions and beliefs, and trying to view things from new or others' perspectives to see if your own beliefs hold true. To do this successfully requires us to have a learner mindset and be inquisitive about what is going on around us, rather than processing everything on the basis of our assumptions.

To discover the deep drivers of our thinking and our mental models, I have found that 'listening' for our defensiveness is a useful tool. Being conscious of our defensive moments and processing why we became defensive helps us to understand some of those mental models we are not conscious of.

When we become defensive it doesn't mean our mental model is wrong, it just means that it has been challenged. Of course, unless you are superhuman you probably won't recognise you are defensive until you are in the middle of an argument ... or perhaps later, as you reflect why the conversation went pear-shaped so quickly. Below are some of the ways I ensure I stay conscious of my mental models that might be playing out:

- Remember that even though I may have been in a similar scenario previously, this situation may not be exactly the same (even in circumstances of abuse, people can fall into old patterns of behaviour because they hold a mental model that they did something to deserve it, that they are completely powerless or that the abuser will change).

- Be curious about my own thinking and of those around me, and reflect at various points about what might be influencing that thinking.
- Go outside my comfort zone and experience life and opinions that differ from mine. I then try to process how and why the experience has challenged how I think life should work.

Now that you are in the place to test your assumptions with a learner mindset, let's see why the change doesn't seem to be occurring as you would like. The first thing I would do is list all the reasons why you cannot change (or don't seem to be having success). It is important to explore the reality of these reasons.

I find the 'Five Whys' a useful and simple exercise for testing assumptions. This process originated with Taiichi Ohno, the inventor of the Toyota Production System and 'lean manufacturing system', in an effort to understand both the underlying problems and solutions involved with manufacturing on a large scale. Asking 'Why?' at the end of each question will eventually lead you to identifying an underlying reason why something isn't happening and offer a possible solution.

Here are a couple of examples:

I just can't seem to find the time to exercise even though I know it is important.

1. I am finding it very hard to exercise: *Why?*
2. I just don't have the time that I would like to commit. *Why?*
3. There are too many demands on my time. *Why does exercise not rate as highly as these?*
4. Exercise is the easiest activity to leave out, as it seems selfish. *Why does it seem selfish?*
5. It is about me and I need to put others first.

So, the reason you are not exercising has nothing to do with time but rather a belief that others must always come first. This belief is what needs to shift – not the exercise behaviours. Until you fundamentally believe that you have the right to do things for yourself, you won't actually shift your exercise habits successfully.

I just don't seem to be able to find a partner who I want to stay in a relationship with.

1. I seem to end up in relationships with people who are controlling. *Why?*
2. I think I'm attracted to strong personalities. *Why?*
3. It makes me feel confident and that someone is in control. *Why is this important?*
4. Because it is important to feel secure. *Why do you need someone for that?*
5. Probably because I am not confident in providing security for myself.

So, the reason you end up with controlling partners may be that you lack confidence in yourself rather than being attracted to strong personalities. Sounds to me like some work needs to be done on yourself first to better understand your own strengths and value.

Here are some other questions to ponder to discover what it is that you may or may not be prepared to give up. Again, if you want to dig deeper, check out the transition plan at the end of the book for an approach that I find to be incredibly helpful in arriving at your core reasons for not changing.

- What small steps could you take in the direction towards your goal or preferred future?
- What are the excuses that keep coming up? Why do these excuses keep reappearing? What would the possible benefits be if you did things differently? What would be the worst that could happen if you did something new?
- Do you have beliefs you know you are not prepared to give up? What are these? Why are they so important to you?
- What assumptions do you hold about how life should work? What evidence do you have that your assumptions are correct? What evidence can you find to point to the fact that your assumptions may not always be correct? (This does not negate the fact that they are correct sometimes.)
- What are those things (behaviours, values) in your life that you may need to give up or stop in order to move towards your desired direction? What will get in the way of you giving these things up?

I invite you now to be really honest with yourself and complete the following tables:

What I won't give up
1.
2.
3.
4.
5.

Impact of not giving these up
1.
2.
3.
4.
5.

Am I okay with those results?
1.
2.
3.
4.
5.

What I am prepared to give up?
1.
2.
3.
4.
5.

Potential impact of giving these things up
1.
2.
3.
4.
5.

LET'S RECAP:

What am I prepared to give up?

- Successful transitions occur when we give up beliefs or behaviours that prevent us moving into our preferred future, even if they have served us well to this point.
- Willpower on its own is never enough to sustainably embed the change we are looking for.
- Life is always about choices and trade-offs. Successful transitions are about making these choices in alignment with our identity and where we would like to be headed.
- Successful transitions often require us to challenge assumptions about what we believe about ourselves, life, and what is possible for us.
- A humble learner mindset is required to do things differently. Arrogance is the belief and behaviour of those who believe that a different life can be lived by doing the same things that they have always done.

What do I need to do to get to my preferred future?

We have spent some time unpacking you! It can be a painful and frustrating journey, and I would like to acknowledge your resilience in staying the course and arriving at the fifth and final key question. Many quit before now, as the process can be confronting. And, let's be honest, sometimes we just don't feel like we have the energy.

To those who have persevered, the good news is you will now have all the pieces in play to move forward. The bad news is that the pieces on their own are not sufficient (I am good at this motivational stuff, aren't I?).

I could promise you that having all the correct pieces means the journey will be easy, but that would be setting you up for failure. There are no magic pills. Just like having all the bricks for building a house doesn't mean you have a house – or buying all the ingredients for a cake doesn't mean you have a cake – having all the pieces for your preferred future doesn't mean you will automatically get there.

But having the correct pieces is *important*. If I want to bake a dairy-free, gluten-free, preservative-free cake (yes, I am serious, and yes, it is a really tasty cake), I need to have the correct ingredients, otherwise my masterpiece will turn out like something else. If you have spent some time working through and processing the previous questions, you will most probably have the correct elements (or at least the essential ones). Now we need to put them together.

Sam puts it all together: closing the gap

In my last session with Sam, I acknowledged her courage in stepping into some uncomfortable territory and asked how she was travelling.

'You know, I feel like I have a chance to do this well,' she said. 'For the first time I feel like I have actually paused and taken hold of the gift in the moment. The last six months has allowed me to breathe and come up for air. Life has still been hectic, but the questions have stuck with me, and I have found myself pondering them at odd times. I was at a party and found myself by the pool thinking about my values. And the other day, as I was picking up groceries, I was processing whether I'm happy with the gap in my life.'

After she finished, I leaned in and said, 'I am so glad that you now have a vision for your preferred future. These visions can often be exciting and a little scary, but that's the nature of seeing what your life could be. You seem to understand where you currently are and the gaps that exist. You better understand your value and who you are.

'You now have the pieces to start building your pathway to your preferred future. You have taken the time to understand what is important to you, your core beliefs and commitments, and who you wish to be.

'Now the work starts.'

Yep, it's that time. Time to look at how you are going to close the gap.

Setting off on a journey requires you to have some idea of where you are headed (unless you are just going to wing it and see what happens). A saying I know of sums this up perfectly:

'Tomorrow: The place where productivity and motivation are believed to reside.' –Anon

Today is the day when I start walking towards my preferred pathway. Tomorrow is the place of dreamers; today is the place of action. Your preferred future begins to form by what you do today!

The Okinawa Centurion Study was established in 1975 and is the longest study of centenarians in the world. For over 48 years researchers have been following the people of Okinawa, Japan, to discover what leads to their longevity and happiness.

The Okinawans follow a lifestyle that includes such habits as only eat until you are 80 per cent full, surround yourself with good friends, do gentle exercise every day, reconnect with nature and follow your *Ikagai* each day.

According to the people of Okinawa, *Ikagai* is where our passion, mission, profession and vocation align. In other words, where we do what we love, what we are good at, what the world needs and what we are being paid for. This is the sweet spot where our true happiness lies.

Sounds great, but is it possible?

Setting the GPS for your new life

I would like to suggest that our preferred destination is both possible and within our grasp. We just need to set our life GPS for the pathway to that destination and then stay focused on our journey. Sometimes we can get caught up with identifying the whole road map. This can get us in trouble as we try to plan every step and either miss out on unexpected surprises or get sideswiped by unexpected events. I think that there are three types of paths that we can set ourselves in pursuit of our new life:

Pathway 1: Where the destination and route is clear.

Pathway 2: Where the destination is clear but the route is not.

Pathway 3: Where neither the destination nor the route is clear.

Pathway 1: Straight-line goals (The destination and route are clear)

There are some areas in life where I can set a plan based on a goal and walk in a straight line towards that goal. For example, I decide that I want to lose weight for a friend's wedding in eight weeks. That is a straight-line goal. I set the goal, make a plan and then stick to it. I decide I want to have a psychology degree. I go to university, study hard and, at some point, pop out with the result. The pathway for both these goals is primarily in my control; there is a clear cause-and-effect relationship.

These are the goals we set ourselves where we are very clear about the goal or outcome and there is really only one way to get there.

Losing weight requires a decrease in calories (i.e. diet) and an increase in energy output (i.e. exercise). While there may be a variety of ways I can do this, there is a linear path between my current state and my goal. If I leave school and wish to become an engineer, I need to study, complete the required units and, if successful, graduate with a certificate in engineering. My pathway to that point may waver all over the place, but once I have made the decision then there is a straight pathway.

These goals don't need to be overcomplicated. If you find yourself not taking the straight pathway, it may be an indication you are not that committed to achieving the goal (this happens a lot more than we would care to admit).

Pathway 2: All roads lead to Rome goal (The destination is clear but there are a few roads I could take)

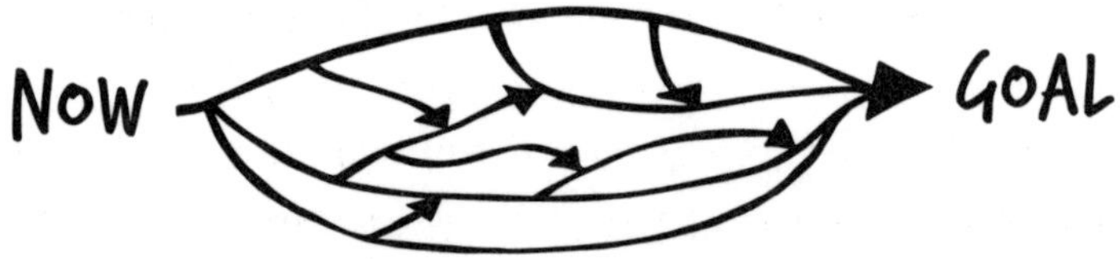

There are other goals I set where there may be multiple pathways to get there but, essentially, I know where I want to arrive. For example, I do a large amount of leadership coaching and work on strategic culture-change projects. I have always had a belief that a well-operating system with the right people can achieve amazing results. I am not unique in that view among others who do similar work to mine. There is not one perfect way to develop the capability to coach others in this type of work.

My pathway to being able to do this work was through a few different career pathways: studying leadership, completing a post-graduate degree in organisational psychology, and then undertaking a PhD in unpacking leadership attributes of healthy high performers. Others who do this same work have got there through their own different, unique pathways. I always knew this was what I wanted to do, but was not entirely clear about the best way to do it. I had an end goal in mind but not the pathway.

In Sam's case, she was seeking the restoration of a relationship with a family member: this is a clear goal. However, the pathway towards that goal was not always clear, so she tried a few different strategies but always with the end goal in mind.

I know of a friend who has the life goal to establish a foundation that will be an extravagant supporter of philanthropic causes and managed by the next generation of their family. They have a clear goal, but there is not a straight-line path to that point. There will be a number of paths taken on their journey to that point. They have begun by making a few very good investments, found willing causes and partnered with like-minded people. And so the path continues.

Each of these stories has one thing in common: moving forward to a clear destination, but taking multiple paths to get there.

Career goals sometimes fit into this category. You may wish to take on a senior management role but need to be open to choosing a few different paths to get there. In most organisations, promotion to senior leadership has become more sophisticated than a straight-line pathway (though unfortunately this model still exists). You may have to accept different roles, work in different locations, take on a variety of projects or enrol in talent programs – but all done with a clear view of the goal.

Pathway 3: Spaghetti bolognese (I have an idea of my preferred future but no idea how to get there)

Then there are nebulous goals or pathways to a preferred future. I may wish to achieve significant influence, an executive career, invent something revolutionary, make a positive impact on those around me, live a fulfilled life or just use my talents in an interesting manner. These are still serviceable as end goals ... provided I am careful not to see a fixed pathway to that preferred future.

Often these end goals emerge out of trying different things, being open to experience, taking risks and the right opportunity emerging at the right time. Momentum is important in these instances; ever notice how lucky people seem to find luck, whereas those who claim they are unlucky seem to have plenty of experiences to support their lack of luck? Not every answer for a recalibrated life fits into this last category, but some do.

I am not talking about a 'que sera, sera' or a 'leave my life up to the winds of change' approach. Sometimes we have no idea where we want to get to or what we want out of life; we just know we want something better. The problem is that too often we live with this gnawing feeling for our whole lives, having at some point resigned ourselves to the fact that our lot in life is settled.

One of my favourite holiday experiences has been visiting Venice with my family. It was around Christmas and it was cold and wet, but hey, I was still in Venice, a lifelong dream of mine. Out of the three of us, I am the organised one. Planning out each day of the holiday makes perfect sense to me so that I can fit in everything I want to do and make sure I squeeze the most out of the experience. Others in my life have that gift of going with the flow and experiencing life as it happens.

Holidays, therefore, are experienced differently by each of us – but, somehow, we manage to find that balance between my organisation and the 'Let's see what happens' approach. On this day our guide told us we were free to wander, and so my first reaction was to look at my tour notes and figure out an ideal day of experiences. I was very happy to try a few things, but they had to be on a list.

My wife's approach was: 'Why don't we just wander and see what happens?'

If you know the islands of Venice, there are many paths all over the place, and if you are not careful you can find yourself wandering aimlessly.

But wander we did – and in doing so, experienced all the beauty of Venice in those few hours. Popping into a pizzeria for a slice of pizza, eating gelato in some back street, finding a ***ristorante*** where I think we were the only ones who spoke English. Yes, it rained, but it was a magical experience because we would just follow a path and see where it took us. There were some streets that led nowhere and others that led to those magical experiences.

This 'preferred future' way of walking towards goals is a bit like my Venice experience. We take hold of the next opportunity with vigour, but have no idea whether that path will lead to a preferred future or a dead end where we need to choose a new path.

Rather than just 'winging it', we approach each path with a plan and preparation, even though we don't know what the end goal is. Rather than setting a goal and walking towards it, we take the next path and find ourselves walking towards a future we may or may not have envisaged.

In your career you may choose to take on a marketing role and then decide to move on and take on an HR role. Why? Not because you want an HR role specifically, but because you want to experience a range of careers and wish to see what may emerge. You work hard in the marketing role and upskill yourself as necessary. Likewise, you do the same with the HR career; but not because you are wanting to be an HR or marketing professional – these are simply careers you are trying out on your journey to a preferred career, one that you may not yet be able to describe or see.

Can I re-emphasise that this approach is not merely wandering through life aimlessly; you are being purposeful in your actions, just without a specific end goal in mind. Each path taken is another experience that feeds into that ultimate goal you have for yourself.

This type of approach generally opens up unforeseen opportunities and experiences, but it requires you to be open to the idea that the preferred future is unknown. It is not to say this approach is better than the other two. We need to practise each of the approaches to achieve what we want out of life. We just need to be clear which approach we are using and act accordingly.

Before you think this type of existence is a loopy, off-with-the-fairies one, it is important to note it requires a high level of insight. If you have not dug deep into the previous questions I have posed, then you are probably not ready for this type of goal setting.

This preferred future pathway involves lots of reflection along the way to ensure lessons are learnt along each of the pathways. It involves the deliberate act of seeking feedback and processing that feedback, rather than blindly wandering down paths. It involves the strength and wisdom to recognise when a path has completed its course and to find a new path.

Often this process requires the help of a critical friend, coach or advisor; someone who knows you well and can prompt and provide opportunities for reflection. It is not a freewheeling 'see what happens' approach to life, but rather a deliberate approach where pathways are tried and connections made to arrive at the preferred future.

How do I know which pathway to choose, then?

When I ask the 'What do I want out of life?' question, I need to be clear on the type of goal I am setting.

Confusion reigns when I set myself a 'preferred future' type of goal and then proceed to implement a straight-line pathway towards that goal. I am most probably setting myself up for early failure. Likewise, if it is a straight-line goal and I approach it with a 'preferred future' pathway, then I may be setting myself up to fail. The reality is that we will probably have different pathways in place for different goals.

Sounds tiring, doesn't it?

However, being clear about the type of goal and pathway makes it easier. In Sam's desire to 'fix' a relationship with a family member, it was not a clear pathway, so we know for this one she would just have to try different things to arrive at the destination.

This takes some pressure off us to have to use the 'right' strategy. For example, I don't know what career I want, but I know I want to do something that excites me. In this case I am happy to explore and see what exotic destination I arrive at. This takes pressure off me having to find the perfect job right now.

This process of selecting pathways is not about changing your whole life. Rather, it is about shifting your thinking and behaviours in small steps. Baby steps will change your life! Our neural pathways are deeply ingrained, and it's hard to get off those highways we have created based on past behaviour and thinking. The longer you have been doing the same thing, the deeper a pathway is embedded into your psyche.

Some of us only have one story to tell ourselves. When we try to change the script, our mind overrides any attempt we make to change and tells us that the old way is better. We have to create new stories – and the only way to do this is to start small. Remember when you started reading? *The Great Gatsby* was not the first book on your reading list; it was probably a book with a few words on each page.

As you developed your reading skills and confidence you progressed, and now you can read without pictures (though sometimes watching the movie helps). Changing behaviours is similar; we start small, grow in confidence and, before we know it, the new us emerges.

It all begins with staying focused

One habit I have that often annoys those close to me (yes, I really can only think of one) is my consistent inconsistency. I make a coffee for my wife most mornings when we are home together. You would think that after over 20 years of wedded bliss I could make the same coffee twice. As my wife often reminds me after an extra strong or weak coffee: 'Why don't you make it the same way every morning?'

She has a point!

I find consistency in habit to be both rewarding and restricting at the same time. If there are multiple ways to arrive at a destination, you can be sure I have tried each one ... just to make sure that mine is the quickest or best. I mean, I would hate to find out after taking one route for a few days or years that a better alternative existed.

The problem when we have a preferred destination in mind is that there are often many pathways to get there and we are not sure of the right one to take. If behaviour change or a better future is what you are seeking, my approach to consistency (or rather lack of consistency) will mean you struggle to find that future. Yes, you may have some fun along the way, but the destination will probably remain an elusive dream.

Success follows those who stay focused; those who can be disciplined enough to follow the same pathway until they see reward. Call it habit, ritual, routine or staying away from fads and shiny objects, the result is the same.

Let's pause and think about the type of pathway that you require for the next part of your journey. Capture this somewhere or in the transition plan at the end of the book.

Moving successfully on the pathway: the strategy for eating an elephant

When I was growing up there were a whole bunch of really bad elephant jokes.

> Q: How can you tell if an elephant has been in your fridge?
> A: Footprints in the butter.
>
> Q: How do you fit four elephants in a Mini?
> A: Two in the front and two in the back (obvious, isn't it?).
>
> Q: What do you get when you cross peanut butter with an elephant?
> A: Either peanut butter that never forgets or an elephant that sticks to the roof of your mouth.
>
> Q: How do you eat an elephant?
> A: One bite at a time.

I love the absurd, but the last joke sticks with me for a different reason. It speaks to the power of habit that brings about change. Sustainable, effective change comes from implementing small, doable habits one step at a time.

As human beings, we are commonly fixated on big, substantial changes. Our mantra is often 'If it's worth doing, it's worth doing big' or 'If it doesn't cost us, then it's not worth doing'. While these mantras may be true for monuments and castles, they are not true for life change.

Rarely do big movements in life cause sustainable change. Granted, sometimes they do and sometimes they are necessary, but they are often very difficult to sustain.

> Sustainable, effective change comes from implementing small, doable habits ...

A more successful approach to changing our lives is to set small, doable, bite-sized, realistic targets and implement specific habits that will take us towards these targets. This will create a momentum that leads you towards your destination. Yes, it may look like it will take longer, BUT it will get you there.

Remember when you learnt to walk? No, neither do I, but having watched others do it ... it begins with small tentative baby steps, and, as confidence grows, our old way of moving (crawling) suddenly doesn't look so good. And so it is with our change.

The key to true life transitions: shift, not change

When it comes to activating 'big' change in our lives, it is often doomed to fail from the start. Our brain perceives a big change as a danger to our existence. On an emotional level it may be that our 'emotional immune system' helps protect us from the fallout that can come with change.

In their book *Immunity to Change*, authors Robert Kegan and Lisa Laskow Lahey describe how our emotional need to be protected from disappointment and shame can cause us to move away from those things that we want to do. This is because, at a neurological level, change is often perceived as a threat.

Think about how you behave when you are threatened. You may get sweaty palms, have angry outbursts, develop a fast-beating heart, feel a temptation to run or become frozen on the spot. All these reactions protect us from the danger. These are all fight or flight responses and, interestingly, are often similar to your physiological responses when you feel you are being compelled to change by others.

Your brain is thinking, *'Uh oh, this is going to be hard; it sounds like a threat to life as I know it.'* The fight or flight response kicks in and, despite working hard at the change, rarely are we effective.

Our system goes into meltdown and we work very hard to overcome the urges to go back to life as it was. Within a month (or sometimes less than a week) we have drifted back into all those old behaviours we so desperately wanted to change. Then the negative self-talk kicks in: 'See, knew it was too tough', 'Maybe that future is beyond my ability', and *insert your own excuse here …*

Can I suggest that an alternative approach that has a better chance of success is to shift our behaviours *slightly* rather than trying to change our lives *completely*.

At one time or another, many of us have bought into the old argument that change must be painful or it isn't worth doing (or the other argument, that one magic pill could fix it all). However, a more helpful approach is to pick some small behaviours or ways of thinking that you could shift. A small shift may be the answer to your new life.

If we haven't exercised for a long time, then a daily walk – although it sounds simple – may be too hard for our system. Instead, a walk once a week, or deciding to take the stairs as often as we can, may in fact get us to the preferred future we are looking for. If our brain registers the new behaviour as successful, it is more likely to want to keep doing the behaviour.

Gradual shifts over time are the answer to a changed life. While it may take a bit longer, it will definitely take less time than continually giving up and restarting.

Vincent van Gogh said: 'Great things are done by a series of small things brought together.' He embraced the truth that a great life is built on the consistency of small disciplines and wise decisions.

Gradual shifts over time are the answer to a changed life. While it may take a bit longer, it will definitely take less time than continually giving up and restarting.

Setting great habits

There is a lot of information about habits already widely available and so I won't go into great detail here. However, remember it is the setting and following of habits that will help you be successful, rather than having a strong theoretical knowledge of habits. Here are a couple of tips that will help you on the journey.

Set yourself up to succeed

Humans have a curious trait when it comes to setting goals. We think that unless it is impossible or very difficult, the goal is not worth setting. We have been told to shoot for the stars, aim high, set ourselves BHAGs (you might like to google this!), and while this is true in terms of what we are aiming for, it is not very useful advice for reaching those goals.

Our brains are hardwired to move towards success and reward, and away from threat and change. When we set those large, sometimes barely achievable goals we set ourselves up to fail from that moment. It is far more pragmatic and ultimately more successful to set small goals and, as we achieve them, set new small goals. Before we know it, that elephant has been eaten and our preferred future awaits us.

We also need to set up habits we believe in and that are in line with our personal values and our unique strengths. If you are not a highly scheduled and structured person, habits that require this type of discipline will quickly fade away. If you are more extroverted, spending hours on your own will probably not lead to success.

There is not a one-size fits all model. This is why Key Question 3, 'What are my strengths?', on page 61, is so important.

Remember, you don't have as much willpower as you think

As children we are taught that if we work hard and focus enough, we can achieve whatever we put our minds to. So if we are going to change our life, that means a lot of hard work, right? Kind of. If it only took hard work and Jedi-like mind strength, we would all be living our preferred future, or at least wandering around trying to move objects with our Jedi powers. The reality is our mind is like any muscle, and at some point it does have a stop button.

The message we were fed as kids that hard work alone will change the world or bring us closer to our goals is not grounded in science. It is grounded more in parents trying to motivate their children (which is a kind of art on its own ... not a science ... but I digress).

Remember, willpower is actually a limited resource when it comes to behaviour change. We have willpower, just not in spades. So hard work within the realms of our available willpower will set us up for success and stop us chasing too many shiny objects. We are more likely to succeed when we focus on only a couple of small shifts at a time, rather than trying to apply willpower to every area of our life and completely running out of steam.

Design your life for success

As BJ Fogg says in *The Tiny Small Habits that Change Everything*: 'Design crushes willpower.'

It is an interesting phenomenon that no matter our intention, we generally default to what is most convenient.

For example, if I have a packet of crisps in the cupboard, I am probably going to eat them – but if the crisps are in a bowl on the bench, I will probably most definitely eat them. If I have to go to the local shops to purchase them, then the probability of me eating them decreases. On a side note, this is why all the 'good' food (by good I mean unhealthy but tasty) is often close to the cash register. We can use this to our advantage as well. If I wish to renew a friendship with an old mate, then placing his number in my phone will increase my chances of calling him – but if I set a calendar appointment on my phone with his phone number in the notes, I am more than likely to call him.

> Every journey begins with a first step, and every journey requires multiple steps. Unless you travel the distance, you won't get there.

A useful piece of advice I once read explains how three simple behaviours can improve our chances of success. There are many articles written about how successful people design their morning routine to set themselves up for success. Simply having three or four repeatable behaviours in the morning can turn your life around. Preparing for these the night before dramatically increases the likelihood of you implementing these.

For example, if you wish to use the gym in the morning, placing your exercise gear out the night before will decrease the preparation you have to do and increase the chances that you will make it to the gym. If you wish to take some time for reflection in the morning, placing your journal in the location you will use increases the likelihood you will engage in this behaviour. If you want to get up early you can place your alarm clock away from your bed, forcing you to get up to turn it off. (Negotiate this with your partner first or your morning may start off on the wrong foot.)

Set small, specific goals

Now we understand the futility of trying to change our world all in one go, let's look at the power of developing achievable habits that will move us towards our preferred future.

Every journey begins with a first step, and every journey requires multiple steps. Unless you travel the distance, you won't get there.

The journey to your preferred destination is best thought of in the same way. What are the steps you need to take? What is a short-term and specific goal you could set yourself to move towards your preferred journey? These are not the necessarily the same habits you will have in a few months' time as you get closer to your goal; they are the habits you need right now that will get your journey underway.

I want to be healthy and energised, so the habits I set now are about getting the journey started. 'I will quit sugar' (harder than you think), 'I will only have a wine on the weekend', and 'I will start walking twice a week' are all small beginner habits building towards my preferred future of being healthy. It definitely sounds far sexier to say 'I will only eat meat and vegetables', 'I will quit alcohol completely' or 'I will run 5 kilometres every day'. These habits for many require so much willpower and are so far removed from current reality that they will not last for long.

Smarty pants habits: ones that actually work

As boring as it sounds, setting a SMART habit will set us up for success. A SMART habit is one that is specific, measurable, achievable, relevant and time-bound.

This could look like:

- I will eat my meals for the next four weeks without adding any sugar. This is a specific action – not adding sugar; measurable – I either did or didn't add sugar; achievable – I think I can put away the sugar bowl but not eating food with sugar may be a step too far right now; relevant – because my doctor told me to cut down on sugar; and time-bound – for the next month.

- Over the next month I will sit at a café and spend 30 minutes on a Tuesday and Friday morning before work reflecting on the question: 'How did I use my strengths yesterday?' This is a specific action – sitting at a café and on specific mornings; measurable – I either did or didn't sit and reflect on the specific question; achievable – because I have a café near work and I can leave 30 minutes early on those two mornings; relevant – because I need to develop my focus on strengths; and time-bound – because I have set myself 30 minutes twice a week for a month.

While these are not world-changing habits, they are journey-starting steps. Success at this level will enable me to take the next step to my preferred future. Yes, I may feel like I am on a slow journey, but the story of the hare and the tortoise rings true here: 'Slow and steady wins the race!'

Review progress regularly

Habits are a bit like training a new puppy. They require lots of reinforcement and checking that you are on the right track. If left unattended, new habits can simply disappear (or you can develop unwanted ones!).

The new habits require that you check in with them regularly to make sure you are putting them into play (just like you need to check in regularly with the new puppy to make sure it is doing what you are training it to do).

When setting up your habits, initially set short-term check-ins. This means you can spot very quickly when habits are starting to deviate or you are reverting to the old behaviours. Check in as regularly as you need, to ensure you stay on track.

Get an accountability buddy

Life was not made to be lived in isolation and nor are new habits implemented in a vacuum.

While the sudden emergence of the 'new you' makes for a great story at a party, rarely are we able to achieve our life plans on our own. When kicking off a new habit, it makes a lot of sense to let someone else know, someone who will help keep you on track. Finding that person who will be just irritating enough not to let you get away with brushing them off is the trick. A friend who doesn't push you too hard is just as effective as one who won't let up.

Sharing your plans with someone else makes you more accountable in following through with your new behaviour. They can help keep you on track and maybe even provide some support as you go about this behaviour change.

Keep at it

In the words of Winston Churchill: 'Never give up.'

Yep, some willpower will be involved to stick at that thing you have decided to do. You will muck it up and slip back, but remember you are on a forward progression. It is a cliché, but sometimes we feel like it is one step forward and ten back. That's normal – just keep pushing forward.

Remember the race is won at the finish line. The winner is never declared at the starting blocks (even if there is a clear favourite, because things can happen along the way). Your new habit is like that – keep going, keep trying and life will be different.

Let's get down to business and reset, review, reacquaint and then recalibrate as needed.

Just like Sam did, it's time to put the plan into action. Time to emerge from this transition process triumphantly.

Like Sam, you have paused and taken stock of the moment. You have reflected deeply on all of the five key questions.

1. Where am I headed ... and am I happy with that?
2. What do I want out of life?
3. What are my strengths?

4. What am I prepared to give up?
5. What do I need to do to get to my preferred future?

I encourage you to not just make this another book that you have read or listened to, but to use the tools provided and *do* something.

The last words I left Sam with are the same that I would like to leave you.

If it is all sounding too hard or overwhelming, it is important to remember that over time most people regret inaction rather than action.

Research by psychologist Tom Gilovich and expert in negotiation and decision-making Professor Vicki Medvec, found that time is a key factor when it comes to our regrets. We usually regret our actions over the short-term. But over the long haul, we tend to regret inactions. Their study found that in an average week, regrets about actions taken (53 per cent) were slightly greater than regrets about actions not taken (47 per cent). But when people looked at their lives over a longer period of time, regrets about actions not taken (84 per cent) outnumbered regrets about actions taken (16 per cent).

Slow down and enjoy the journey (but keep going)

I remember debriefing a director at the completion of a project he'd been leading, which had been a hard slog for all involved. While the team delivered the final product, it was over budget and behind schedule. It was a bruising encounter to say the least. When I asked him what he had learnt and what he would do differently, he told me that he would have pressed pause earlier and reset the team. When I asked him why, he said, 'We were so busy and under pressure that we thought we just had to keep going.' In hindsight, taking a week to reset would have saved them much money, time and unnecessary stress.

When we think about our lives, it is important to think about our preferred futures. Often, reassessment of our lives stems from our realisation that we are not heading towards our preferred future but away from it. Of course, we aren't always aware that we're not heading towards our preferred future; we just have a sense that we might be on the wrong track.

At some point, you have to decide whether to keep going or retrace your steps. Transitions are a bit like this feeling of growing unease. They are an opportunity to stop and evaluate where we are. To reacquaint ourselves with our lives and decide to keep on the same path or shift direction ... to reset our pathway.

I know that when I am driving somewhere and realise I am lost, the dumbest thing I could do would be to keep driving and just hope I work things out. If I am smart, I will stop, take out my phone and look at my maps to get my bearings. Although we know this about simple things like driving, for those more complicated issues like *living* we tend to stumble blindly on and wonder why we end up in the wrong location.

The global pandemic has provided us all with the opportunity to pause life and check our roadmap for where we are going. Unfortunately, some will keep driving without pausing ... I encourage you to be among the thoughtfully courageous.

As we finish this part of our journey together, I also encourage you to enjoy the process.

My brother and I went on many road trips as young adults and would generally have a great time. One thing that used to bug me about my brother, however, was that he wanted to pull over at every service station and every road stop, and deviate through all the small country towns. My view was that our holiday started when we arrived at our destination. We were both frustrated. Being the gentle, compromising soul that I am, we generally stopped at a few places but got to our destination within my time frame.

> I would encourage you to pause every so often and ask yourself what matters when it comes to your relationships, finances, work, health, spiritual self and your important causes.

I would like to think that I have learnt to slow down and be in the moment, but a recent morning walk with my wife as I was writing this book reminded me how hardwired I tend to be about moving quickly.

I treat these walks as exercise, meaning I like to keep moving in a forward direction without stopping. My wife, on the other hand, as an artistic person, can't help but stop and capture the beauty with her camera.

On this particular morning I was powering on as normal, when I heard a squeal of delight. I turned around and there, close to the stone wall holding back the river, were a couple of dolphins, slowly cruising. My first thought was 'What a great view,' and then I turned around and kept powering on. It slowly dawned on me that this was one of those 'Be in the moment and enjoy what is happening' opportunities.

Yes, I am a slow learner, but I did stop – and then watched these beautiful creatures putting on a spectacular show for us. It reminded me that those people who focus only on the outcome miss many life-changing moments along the way.

I would encourage you to pause every so often and ask yourself what matters when it comes to your relationships, finances, work, health, spiritual self and causes that are important to you.

I leave you with these words that Ray Kroc (who was responsible for the global expansion of McDonald's) had on his wall to inspire him:

> *Nothing in the world can take the place of persistence.*
>
> *Talent will not; nothing is more common than unsuccessful men with great talent.*
>
> *Genius will not; unrewarded genius is almost a proverb.*
>
> *Education will not; the world is full of educated derelicts.*
>
> *Persistence and determination alone are omnipotent.*
>
> US President Calvin Coolidge

Enjoy the journey!

LET'S RECAP:

What do I need to do to get to my preferred future?

- Being clear about the type of goal you have set yourself and the kind of pathway (straight line; all roads lead to Rome; or spaghetti bolognese) makes it easier to realise which one to take.

- Rarely do big movements in life cause sustainable change. A more successful approach to changing our lives is to set small, doable, bite-sized, realistic targets and implement specific habits that will take us towards these targets.

- The key to true life transitions: shift, not change

- Willpower is actually a limited resource when it comes to behaviour change. Habits override willpower.

- Make SMART goals and get an accountability buddy.

My transition plan

What's your transition moment? Take a little time to write down your impetus to press pause. Is it a deliberate pause or has it been forced upon you by some life event? This is an opportunity to process whether you are in the starting blocks ready to start the journey, or still making your way to the starting blocks. Any position is fine, just be honest with yourself.

- What is the transition moment you feel or think you are in now?
- Where is the gift for you in this transition moment?
- What does embracing this transition moment mean for you?
- What would you like to believe, achieve or be once you have moved through this transition moment?
- Do you have any pressing deadlines or priorities you need to consider as you start this process?

Key Question 1: Where am I headed ... and am I happy with that?

Read through the following questions and take some time to write what comes to mind as you reflect.

- How does your current work/job line up with what you want out of life (your why)?
- How would you describe your closest relationships?
- Who are your friends?
- What is the state of your physical health?
- What is your personal impact on those around you?
- Do you have awareness of your spiritual world?
- Are you financially where you wish to be?
- What is the state of your emotional health?

Use the following tables to help reflect on any gaps in your world.

FINANCE

WHAT IF ...

What would you like to spend your money on?

WHAT IS YOUR CURRENT REALITY? *(The more honest you can be, the more likely you are to successfully move through a transition.)*

What are you actually spending your money on?

THE GAP *(What is the gap between what you would like and the current reality? Be as specific as possible.)*

TIME

WHAT IF ...

Where would you like your time to go?

WHAT IS YOUR CURRENT REALITY? *(The more honest you can be, the more likely you are to successfully move through a transition.)*

Where does your time go?

THE GAP *(What is the gap between what you would like and the current reality? Be as specific as possible.)*

FAMILY

WHAT IF ...

How would you like to be described by those closest to you?

WHAT IS YOUR CURRENT REALITY? *(The more honest you can be, the more likely you are to successfully move through a transition.)*

How would those closest to you describe you?

THE GAP *(What is the gap between what you would like and the current reality? Be as specific as possible.)*

FRIENDS

WHAT IF ...

What would you like your relationships to look and feel like?

WHAT IS YOUR CURRENT REALITY? *(The more honest you can be, the more likely you are to successfully move through a transition.)*

What do your relationships actually look and feel like?

THE GAP *(What is the gap between what you would like and the current reality? Be as specific as possible.)*

WORK

WHAT IF ...

How would you like your peers and colleagues to describe you?

WHAT IS YOUR CURRENT REALITY? *(The more honest you can be, the more likely you are to successfully move through a transition.)*

How would your peers and colleagues describe you?

THE GAP *(What is the gap between what you would like and the current reality? Be as specific as possible.)*

LEADERSHIP

WHAT IF ...

What would you like your staff or colleagues say about you when you aren't around?

WHAT IS YOUR CURRENT REALITY? *(The more honest you can be, the more likely you are to successfully move through a transition.)*

What would they say about you when you aren't around?

THE GAP *(What is the gap between what you would like and the current reality? Be as specific as possible.)*

ENVIRONMENT

WHAT IF ...

What impact would you like to make on the environment?

WHAT IS YOUR CURRENT REALITY? *(The more honest you can be, the more likely you are to successfully move through a transition.)*

What impact do you have on the environment?

THE GAP *(What is the gap between what you would like and the current reality? Be as specific as possible.)*

HEALTH

WHAT IF ...

How would you like to describe your health?

WHAT IS YOUR CURRENT REALITY? *(The more honest you can be, the more likely you are to successfully move through a transition.)*

How would you describe your health?

THE GAP *(What is the gap between what you would like and the current reality? Be as specific as possible.)*

SPIRITUAL

WHAT IF ...

If you had a spiritual component to your life, what would it be?

WHAT IS YOUR CURRENT REALITY? *(The more honest you can be, the more likely you are to successfully move through a transition.)*

Is there a spiritual component to your life?

THE GAP *(What is the gap between what you would like and the current reality? Be as specific as possible.)*

OTHER AREAS?

WHAT IF ...

WHAT IS YOUR CURRENT REALITY? *(The more honest you can be, the more likely you are to successfully move through a transition.)*

THE GAP *(What is the gap between what you would like and the current reality? Be as specific as possible.)*

Key Question 2: What do I want out of life?

Are there stories about yourself that you have believed, which have sent you down a path that is possibly not the right one for you? (Remember, these stories could have been encouraging or discouraging, but were not congruent with what is important to you.)

What do you care about? What would you like to see done differently in your family, relationships, work, the world?

Describe how you would like your life to be in a few years' time (time span up to you). What would you be doing? Who would you be around? What would you not be doing? How would life be different to what it is now?

If you could change something right now about your reality, something that is in your power to change, what would that be? Why would you want to change that?

Key Question 3: What are my strengths?

This question covers your unique strengths and aspects of your personality that can either help or hinder you.

How am I wired?

- What were your top three values? (See www.personalvaluesgames.com if you need help working out your values.)
- How would you use these values to describe yourself?
- Circle the words you chose out of the personality categories. (A website like www.16personalities.com can be of use here.)

- How would you use these categories to describe yourself?
- What guides your decision making?
- How does this help you live your life more fully?
- What do your guiding principles need to be for this next period of your life?

Think about these as you construct your own guidelines:

- What is most important to focus on for the period of time? (This time frame is at your discretion, depending on your goals and comfort in letting things go for a while. It is important to try and limit areas of importance to four or five, otherwise you are probably trying to fit too much in and not really setting yourself priorities.)
- Be careful not to make the guidelines so general or vague that you could fit any request into them. Guidelines that are too specific may not help either, as they may become a to-do list (which very few of us find liberating or inspirational). Remember, you are trying to create guidelines for decision making that will help you make better use of your time.
- Write a list of everything you could do ... then get tough. Ask yourself: 'Do they fit with the priorities?' (You may need some outside help if you are attached to each of the things you could do.)

Putting it all together

Based on your answers above, you may find it useful to spend some time writing about yourself. Describe how you would define the real you. Where do I get my fuel (purpose)? What guides my decision making (values)? How am I wired (personality)?

Key Question 4: What am I prepared to give up?

Sometimes, we don't want to let go of what we know because the future is uncertain. The adage 'better the devil you know than the one you don't' is true for all of us in some area of our life. What are those things you are not prepared to give up? And are they holding you back?

Letting go will involve a level of discomfort, and sometimes you might feel like it is easier to revert to what you know. Moving on is often messy and sometimes very painful; tears will be shed, anger may be experienced, feelings of hopelessness may overwhelm you. Remember it is all for a reason; you are moving towards your preferred future financially, relationally, emotionally, vocationally, spiritually, physically, socially and intellectually.

Of course, none of us have to answer these questions, but the reality is we will stay where we are if we don't.

- What small steps could you take in the direction towards your goal or preferred future?
- What are the excuses that keep coming back? Why? What would the possible benefits be if you did things differently? What would be the worst that could happen if you did something new?
- Do you have beliefs you know you are not prepared to give up? What are these? Why are they so important to you?

- What assumptions do you hold about how life should work? What evidence do you have that your assumptions are correct? What evidence can you find to point to the fact that your assumptions may not always be correct?
- What are the behaviours and values in your life that you may need to give up or stop in order to move towards your desired direction? What will get in the way of you giving these things up?

I invite you now to be honest with yourself and complete the following tables:

What I won't give up
1.
2.
3.
4.
5.

Impact of not giving these up
1.
2.
3.
4.
5.

Am I okay with those results?
1.
2.
3.
4.
5.

What am I prepared to give up?
1.
2.
3.
4.
5.

Potential impact of giving these things up
1.
2.
3.
4.
5.

Key Question 5: What do I need to do to get to my preferred future?

- What is the type of pathway I need to choose to head towards my preferred future: straight line, all roads lead to Rome or spaghetti bolognese?
- Why do I think that this choice of pathway will be the best to help me with my transition?
- What is the first step I need to take on this pathway?
- What are my specific habits going to be to help me move forward? What are one or two achievable behaviours that I could do straight away? How will I know if I am successful?
- When will I check in to see how I am progressing?

My Plan

Reset

- Why do I need to make a transition in my life?

Review

- What is the gap between what I want and where I am?
- What could life look like if I was to make the changes?

Reacquaint

- What are my strengths?
- What is my purpose that will keep me energised?
- What are the one or two guiding principles that will keep me focused?
- What are my guiding principles that will help me keep moving in the right direction?

Recalibrate

- What do I need to give up or stop in order to make the shift?
- What am I prepared to think and do differently in order to be successful?
- What is the type of path I need to take?
- What are the two habits I will do every day to stay on track?
- How will I know that I am successfully doing those two things?
- Who do I need to tell what I am planning to do?

Resources

Ackerman, Courtney (2020). 'What is Self-Awareness?' *Positive Pyschology.com*. https://positivepsychology.com/self-awareness-matters-how-you-can-be-more-self-aware/

Ahmed, Adeel, Arshad, Mohd Anuar, Mahmood, Arshad & Akhtar, Sohail (2016). 'Spiritual intelligence (SQ): A holistic framework for human resource development.' *Revista Administratie Si Management Public* (Romania), 2016 (26), 60–77.

Batterson, Mark (2016). *In a Pit with a Lion on a Snowy Day: How to Survive and Thrive When Opportunity Roars*, Multnomah Press, USA.

Clear, J (2018). *Atomic habits: An easy & proven way to build good habits & break bad ones*, Random House, UK.

Delagran, L (2016). 'Develop Your Spiritual Resources.' www.takingcharge.csh.umn.edu/enhance-your-wellbeing/purpose/spirituality/develop-your-spiritual-resources (University of Minnesota, USA).

Ferris, Timothy (2011). *The 4-Hour Work Week: Escape the 9-5, Live Anywhere and Join the New Rich*, Random House, UK.

Ferris, Timothy (2016). *Tools of Titans: The Tactics, Routines, and Habits of Billionaires, Icons, and World-Class Performers*, Random House, UK.

Furtick, Steven (2014). *Greater: Dream bigger. Start Smaller. Ignite God's Vision for Your Life*, Multnomah Press, USA.

Garcia, H & Miralles, F (2017). *Ikigai: The Japanese Secret to a Long and Happy life*, Random House, UK.

Groeschel, Craig (2017). *Daily Power: 365 Days of Fuel for Your Soul*, HarperCollins Religious, USA.

Jung, C G (1951). *Aion: Researches into the Phenomenology of the Self*, Routledge, UK.

Kegan, R & Lahey, Lisa L (2009). *Immunity to Change: How to Overcome it and Unlock Potential in Yourself and Your Organization*, Harvard Business Press, USA.

Keirsey, David (2006). *Please Understand Me II: Temperament, Character, Intelligence*, Prometheus Nemesis Book Company, USA.

Kofman, Fred (2019). *Conscious Business: How to Build Value Through Values*, St Martins Press, Australia.

Kouzes, James M & Posner, Barry Z (2023). *The Leadership Challenge: How to Make Extraordinary Things Happen in Organizations*, John Wiley & Sons Inc. USA.

Meyer, Pamela (1988). *Agility Shift: Creating Agile and Effective Leaders, Teams and Organisations.* Taylor & Francis, USA.

Ohno, Taiichi (1988). *Toyota Production System: Beyond large-scale production*. Routlege, USA.

Okinawa Research Center for Longevity Science. https://orcls.org/

Ryan, Richard M & Deci, Edward L (2017). *Self-Determination Theory: Basic Psychological Needs in Motivation, Development, and Wellness*, The Guildford Press, USA.

Steriade, M (1996). 'Arousal: Revisiting the Reticular Activating System.' *Science*, 272 (5259), 225–225.

Tedeschi, RG (2020). *Growth after Trauma.* https://hbr.org/2020/07/growth-after-trauma

Acknowledgements

I would like to acknowledge my wife, Monique, who has supported my journey as an author for the last 20 years. Monique epitomises many of the principles in the book and so I feel I have had a close look at reset and transition in action. I am blessed to live life with you.

To my parents, for providing many opportunities to learn and grow.

To Kelly, my business partner, thank you for believing in this dream. We get to have these conversations with people who choose to work with us and I feel blessed to be able to work together the way we do.

To Vanna, Jodene and Nichola, thank you for reading a very early version of the book and giving me hope that I was on the right track. It has taken a while since then but I got there.

To the amazing leaders I get to work with and learn from daily. The trust you place in me will never be taken for granted.

To John and Amanda Maclean, thank you for introducing me to Juliet and being on this journey as we take the message of healthy change to the world.

To Juliet, Diana, Sam, Cherie and the amazing team who have made me look and sound far more professional than I actually am! Thank you for your dedication to this project.

To all the people I have had the privilege of working with as a professional consultant over the years, thank you for your conversations and wisdom.